THE GREAT EXCHANGE

MY JOURNEY
OF SURRENDER AND
LESSONS ALONG THE WAY

Michelle Randall

Foreword by Pastor John Randall
Calvary Chapel San Juan Capistrano

The Great Exchange: My Journey of Surrender and Lessons Along the Way
Second Edition
©2018 by Michelle Randall.

A Daily Walk Publishing
31612 El Camino Real
San Juan Capistrano, CA 92675
949-443-2572

©2018 A Daily Walk Publishing
All Rights Reserved.

www.adailywalk.org

ISBN: 978-0-692-02663-2

Cover Design/Layout: Sarah O'Neal, Designer, Eve Custom Artwork
Back Cover Photograph: Elyse Leedom Photography
Interior Photograph: Heather Kusunoki
About the Author Interior Photograph: Elyse Leedom Photography
Editor: Ali B. Kagamaster

Printed by BELIEVERSBOOKSERVICES in the United States of America.

Foreword

Someone said salvation is the miracle of a moment but sanctification is the process of a lifetime. That process begins when you respond to the words of Jesus, "Follow Me."

When Jesus said, "Follow Me," it meant walk the same road with Him. The narrow road we travel has many ups and downs, twists and turns with obstacles to overcome and battles to fight. But the great news is we do not walk this road alone. We have the promise of the presence of the Holy Spirit every step of the way.

I have had the joy and privilege to walk a portion of my life's journey with Michelle. Her love for the Lord and pursuit of His will for her life has often inspired me to greater heights.

In this book you will discover how The Lord has worked in her life through His Word and by His Spirit bringing her into a deeper love and commitment to Jesus. It is not always easy to exchange our will for Gods will. Yet, it is when we surrender to the Lord and receive what He gives that we truly begin to live the abundant life in Christ.

John Randall, Senior Pastor
Calvary Chapel San Juan Capistrano

Preface

This life is a journey. For Believers, it's a journey with Jesus, made up of various stages of growth: trusting in Jesus, knowing how to grow in our walk, resisting temptation, serving the Lord with our gifts, wallowing through legalism, freed by grace, empowered by the Holy Spirit, learning to step out in faith and do crazy things for Jesus, enduring trials, persevering through prayer, ever patient for His return. I believe this is why Paul said to "work out your salvation" (Philippians 2:12). It is work. Sometimes you may feel as though you are toiling and never gain any ground. Or while fighting in a battle you gain strength and come out victorious. Yet other times you may become fearful, weak and discouraged.

My journey has been going on for many years and the wild ride continues. I'm either hanging on for dear life or soaring like an eagle. There are high highs and low lows. But the higher you go with Jesus, the more awaits you. As you soar high with Him, you see a completely different perspective on life, ministry, parenting, friendship and marriage. The deeper you dive the more you discover about Jesus and yourself. Much like John the Baptist, we echo the words, "He must increase, but I must decrease" (John 3:30).

How do we get to the point of uttering John's words? How do we maneuver through all the muck and mire, the trials, tribulations and demanding expectations often part of this journey called life? I'm prayerful that my experiences, hardships and mistakes will help you in your process of becoming more like Jesus.

My heart and prayer is to cheer you on and encourage you in your quest to complete surrender—that you, too, like me, will be set free as you surrender your will for His, knowing that His will is so much better than anything we could possibly imagine.

Michelle Randall

It is for freedom that Christ has set us free. Stand firm, then, and do not let yourselves be burdened again by a yoke of slavery" (Galatians 5:1).

Contents

1

The Journey Begins

~ learning to eat right ~

I was raised in church but never heard the gospel message presented until 1985 at a Billy Graham Crusade in Anaheim, California. It was as though God spoke right to my heart—like no one else but me was at Angel Stadium. When Billy Graham gave the invitation my response was quick. For the first time in my life I knew that when I died I was going to heaven. This is where my journey with Jesus began, although it would be another four years before I would surrender myself completely to Him.

Then in High School and trying to find my place in the world, I struggled with doing what I knew was right and giving in to what everyone else was doing. Some of my friends had heard about Jesus and started to share what they were learning with me. They invited me to church at Calvary Chapel West Covina, where Raul Reis was pastor. This is where I began to grow. Much like an infant, I started by drinking the spiritual equivalent of milk, then began eating mashed up baby food and finally arrived at solid food. This didn't happen over night. No, it would be four years of being spoon-fed before I was ready to digest spiritual meat of the Word.

Peter encourages us in 1 Peter 2:2 to crave and long for the pure spiritual milk of the Word of God so that we may grow up in our salvation. Much like a child's body matures to the point of digesting food other than milk, our spiritual bodies mature and need more nutrients as well. There is a time for milk and a time for meat.

Hebrews 5:14 says, "But solid food belongs to those who are of full age, *that is*, those who by reason of use have their senses exercised to discern both good and evil," referring to those who are no longer babes. At some point in our walks with the Lord we mature beyond the spiritual milk and our bodies need more nutrients. Meat provides certain nutrients that milk does not. Zinc, Vitamin B_{12}, and COQ10 are found in large quantities of meat and aid in the vital function of our organs.

Likewise, by digging into the Word of God to obtain a healthy portion of *spiritual meat* each day we give our spiritual bodies the correct nutrients to grow to complete maturity. Think about it. I would never give my teenager just milk for breakfast, lunch and dinner. No, a growing child needs more protein to help their maturing body function properly. By not giving them what their body needs they would become anemic and lethargic with stunted growth. The same is true with us as we walk through life with Jesus. Our spiritual body needs the correct nutrients or we will become spiritually malnourished.

Spiritual nourishment comes in different stages. Some of us stay in the infant stage longer than others, depending upon what type of *spiritual diet* we're consuming, When we are full grown we get to enjoy a diet of meat and potatoes. Unfortunately, some never get to this point and stay in the mashed up baby food stage, their palate never acquiring a taste for more.

Why does this happen? Why do some go on and partake of the *meat* and mature spiritually, yet others don't change their diets and therefore stagnate and never reach full growth? I believe it's because many believers are not taught to grow spiritually. Many are not encouraged or instructed to dig deep into the Word of God to let their roots bury themselves within its good healthy soil. Therefore, they remain a mile wide and an inch deep.

In Matthew 13, Jesus shares the parable of the soils. He describes different types of soil and how these represent different hearts of people. Some receive the Lord and it is temporary. Others are glad and initially see a change but the cares of the world quickly snatch their faith away. Still others are planted on good soil and are taught the Word of God, seek daily devotions, pray, stay in continual fellowship and grow, grow, grow. The key is, and always will be, the Word of God. The Word alone produces good soil and provides a healthy balanced *spiritual* diet.

I remember very well going from the *milk of the Word* to the *meat of the Word*, from becoming easily uprooted to deeply rooted. As a new believer the Bible seemed confusing and difficult to understand but the first time the Holy Spirit gave me clear understanding in the Word on my own, no commentary was needed. It was magnificent! I ran to my parents' room early in the morning and excitedly shared my new found treasures that were hidden deep in the Scriptures and then deep within my heart.

When I lived at home with my parents, who were new believers at the time, I experienced great joy sharing with them the treasures that I found in God's Word. It was a season of digging in good soil, watering and planting many seeds. It was also a season of storms.

Soon after you're planted on the good soil and grow, you may—or should I say *you will*, encounter some storms. Believers can count on times of trials and testing. This is God's way of making our faith strong. James 1:2-3 says, "Count it all joy when you enter these trials, knowing the testing of your faith produces patience." And Paul tells us in Romans 5: "We who glory in tribulations, knowing that tribulation produces perseverance, and perseverance character, and character hope (verses 3-4). Trials and testing are necessary for our growth. I've heard it said the Christian is either entering a trial, coming out of a trial, or right in the middle of one.

Trials and tribulations are part of the Christian life whether we like it or not. Though expected, we must endure, knowing that trials produce godly characteristics of perseverance, character and hope. As we go through trials, we can look to the Lord, lean on Him and learn from His Word. Getting to the place of hope with *the expectation of coming good* is truly a blessing. When we can say in the midst of a storm, "This does not move me," we have hope, knowing that God is working out His perfect will in and through our lives. Knowing that He has purpose in our storm, knowing that He does all things for good in our lives as believers (see Romans 8:28), and knowing that He is in control, all lead to hope.

Trees that are planted where fierce winds twist their branches and bend their trunks to the point of nearly breaking are commonly more deeply rooted than those trees growing in a secluded valley where storms never bring any stress or strain. The same is true with us. Our strongest and greatest character is grown through our hardest times, our strongest storms and our times of being bent backward. But, we are not left alone. Jesus promises He is with us, to see us through our storms and even to make us stronger because of them.

The Psalmist knew this well as he wrote: "For You, O God, have tested us. You have refined us as silver is refined. You brought us into the net. You laid affliction on our backs. You have caused men to ride over our heads. We went through fire and through water; but You brought us out to rich fulfillment" (Psalm 66:10-12).

Isn't that how you feel when you are in the midst of a trial, as though you are trapped in a net with a heavy burden on your back? Don't you sometimes feel you are in over your head? The Psalmist describes it well. But, trials don't last forever, praise God! The Lord is faithful to bring us through our trials as He brings rich fulfillment of His perfect plan in our lives while we yield, allowing Him to have His way.

Trials have a way of either making us bitter or better. The enemy knows this well and waits for a time to enter our world to try and draw us away from Jesus through surprise attack: bitterness or fear. The devil always goes after the easy prey, normally the wounded, the weak and the babies in Christ.

Those especially vulnerable to the attacks of the enemy are new believers, those who haven't have had time to get their roots deeply planted and watered into God's Word for protection and direction.

It's a fact that the enemy always goes after easy prey like the wounded, weak and newly saved. Babies especially tend to be slower and not as discerning as adults. The young sea turtle, for example, is particularly vulnerable. As a sea turtle hatches and makes its way to the sea, it goes as fast as its little legs will allow. But, birds instinctively know this and wait patiently for these turtles to hatch. As the young turtles begin to make their way make their way to the sea for safety, that's when the birds attack.

Baby Christians, like those sea turtles, are extremely vulnerable. Not as experienced as mature Christians they are often ignorant of the tactics of the Enemy. The *key* is to get to the water as fast as possible—the *Living Water* that is. Jesus said to the Samaritan women at the well, "*Whoever drinks of this water will thirst again, but whoever drinks of the water that I shall give him will never thirst*" (John 4:13-14).

Do you want to grow in your walk with the Lord? Whether or not you are a new believer, the key remains the same: *be in the Word* (the good soil, the living water) *daily*! The Bible is our nourishment, our water, our milk, our meat and our bread. The Word is what sustains us, quenches our thirst and keeps us going.

When I first became a Christian and really began to walk with the Lord, I couldn't get enough of the God's Word; it really was my food. The Word of God is the only thing that can sustain us, wash us, encourage us, convict us, mold us, shape us and transform us. The Word acts like soap, washing us from the inside out as it goes in. I can't quite explain how it does it—it just does.

As we learn of Him, He changes us. Paul said that "we are transformed by the renewing of [our] mind[s]" (Romans

12:2). The word used here for "transformed" is *metamorphosis*, the same word used for the process that takes place when a caterpillar turns into a butterfly. It's that mysterious, yet beautiful, transformation that takes place through time as the caterpillar changes into the pupa and then into the butterfly.

The same is true with us as believers, except we go from a baby to a teenager and then to an adult. Unlike the butterfly, we never fully arrive at adulthood as believers because we are constantly being transformed into the image of Jesus (see Romans 12:2). This is called sanctification, the process of becoming more and more like Jesus. This process lasts a lifetime and will not be complete until we are in glory with Jesus Himself.

So, what shall we do?

We keep pressing on, transforming, staying in the Word, in prayer, and in fellowship, serving Him and falling more in love with Him each day. We submit, we yield, and we surrender our lives in exchange for His perfect will. As we do these things, **Regarding surrender, A.W. Tozer said, "The reason why many are still troubled, still seeking, still making little forward progress is because they haven't yet come to the end of themselves."** we will find that there is such sweet fellowship in Jesus waiting for a fully surrendered life to Him. Such joy that awaits, such peace that is present and hope that is found in a submitted and surrendered life!

True surrender takes coming to the end of ourselves so He may begin. It takes time, often a lifetime, to complete. "One does not surrender a life in an instant," says Elizabeth Elliott. "That which is lifelong can only be surrendered in a lifetime."

2

Hedged In

~ learning to walk ~

I was raised to be very disciplined, not by my parents—by my coaches. As far back as I can remember I was in the gym. Starting at the age of three at the community recreation center. I, along with my sister (we were only seventeen months apart in age), began a sport that we would grow to love. Looking back now, I see that the Lord taught me so much in my early years through gymnastics. I learned how to stretch before exercise, eat right, work hard, persevere through pain, respect authority, overcome defeat and never give up. I'm thankful for my fifteen years in competitive sports. Aside from teaching me some valuable tools for life I now look back and see that it's how the Lord kept me hedged in. Psalm 139 verses 5 and 6 says: "You have hedged me behind and before, and laid Your hand upon me. Such knowledge is too wonderful for me; it is high, I cannot attain it."

It's humbling to look back at my life before I lived for Jesus. I often marvel how He protected me from harm. How He allowed me to get caught to redirect me. How He allowed my heart to ache to reveal His perfect plan for my life. Though vague then, it's clear now. I knew God had placed His Spirit in me at that Billy Graham crusade back in 1985. I felt different and was convicted for the first time when I sinned. Sinning was no longer pleasurable, it was convicting. Nevertheless, it would be two more years of wavering before I would make the big exchange: my will for His.

But all those years of sports had ingrained something in me: *you can do it if you put your mind to it.* However, there are certain things you cannot do on your own and I was done trying.

In my second year at California State University Long Beach, I was ready to throw in the towel. I was done trying to do it on my own and for the first time in my life I recognized that I needed help. On a Tuesday night in June, 1987, I was divinely led to Calvary Chapel Costa Mesa, where I walked forward for the last time and recommitted my life to Christ.

This was my third time reciting the sinner's prayer, and in my case, the third time was a charm. I plugged into church, moved home, changed colleges, separated from friends, and committed to finish college as soon as possible. I took as many classes as allowed, changed my major from nutrition to child development, and even attended summer school. At twenty-one years old, I graduated with a degree in child development and began teaching fifth grade at Maranatha Christian Academy (MCA), Calvary Chapel Costa Mesa's elementary school.

Looking back, the Lord's hand was all over me as He led and guided me each step of the way. He was the One who instilled in me early on to never give up. He gave me determination, focus and perspective. He opened doors and provided all that I needed. He planned my ways and reveled them to me.

I became a different person with His perspective on life. It was no longer about me. It was about Him and His will for my life. Though several other teaching jobs surfaced that were closer to home, I knew the Lord wanted me to stay at MCA. This would become my teaching ground. Not just as a teacher but as a student. MCA is where Jesus would teach me by example what it meant to be a godly woman.

The Lord surrounded me with seasoned, godly teachers and staff members who took me under their wings to tutor me in godliness, always pointing me to Jesus and the Word of God. This is where I received a crash course in speech, modesty and conduct, all of which I'm so grateful for. My daily prayer was a simple one: "Lord, make me a godly woman. Amen."

It wasn't long before I met a young janitor. He delivered a chair to my classroom and we exchanged a few words. Then, it was paper towels being delivered whether I asked for them or not, and my trash was always being emptied. We talked, met at church, set up chairs together at church, and went to breakfast—and we were engaged nineteen days later!

Reflecting on how the Lord worked in my life at that time, I know now that He needed me to be married—and married quickly—to a godly man who loved Jesus more than me and could lead this strong-willed, stubborn, confident young woman that I was. What I soon found out about my husband is that we have similar personalities. In our case, opposites did not attract! He, too, was heavily involved in sports, singing and performing as a young child. To say he was confident and driven would be an understatement. The last thing he was looking for was a wife, but the Lord knew we needed each other to learn and grow, to sharpen and sand one another. After many years of marriage, I can truly see the Lord's hand in molding and shaping two extremely tenacious people and revealing the benefits of never, ever giving up.

We don't claim to have a perfect marriage but we do claim to serve a perfect God. He has shown us what perseverance, diligence, longsuffering and forgiveness really look like and what the benefits of that are in our marriage.

The key to a godly marriage is simple— *read your Bible every day!* He alone is the glue that keeps a godly marriage together. The key to a godly marriage is simple— *read your Bible every day!* The Word of God will keep us submissive, humble and teachable, molding, shaping and cleansing from the inside out. The Bible is the underlying and overwhelming key that unlocks the blessings of a godly marriage and as a wife, I have learned that the best thing we can do for our husbands is to read the Word daily.

Early on, I realized I couldn't change my husband; only the Holy Spirit can change a person. So, I stopped trying and started praying. I committed to daily reading the Word and that's when everything changed. My heart toward my husband changed and he changed, too. I learned to trust him as he sought the Lord and made decisions. Before my very eyes I witnessed two strong willed, stubborn lives transform into the very image of Jesus Christ.

Though we are far from perfect, we serve a perfect God. We know that as long as we continue to practice the disciplines we've grown to know, we will become more perfected in our lives personally, and in our marriage as the Lord sees fit. With Jesus at the center of our lives and marriage we can get through anything. The key is to keep Him at the center. We may fall down occasionally along the way, but with Him at the center of it all, we are sure to make it through.

Be encouraged today that the Lord is with you. If you have fallen in your walk, get back up and let the Lord lead you once again. He is the God of second chances. He is the One who has hedged

You have hedged me behind and before, And laid Your hand upon me. *Such* knowledge *is* too wonderful for me; It is high, I cannot *attain* it (Psalm 139:5-6).

you in and goes before you. He is the One who is behind you and on each side of you.

3

The Great Exchange

~ learning to surrender ~

It has been decades that I have been in the process of relinquishing my will for His. I've learned many lessons along the way and have grown in my relationship with the Lord. I'm becoming confidant in how God made me unique, allowing Him to work with my personality, gifts, abilities, likes and dislikes, stubbornness and tenacity and even my strong will. Instead of fighting Him, I have surrendered all to Him.

You see, God expects our absolute surrender, and in exchange, He gives us His perfect will. Knowing that we cannot surrender all of ourselves on our own, He slowly and steadily brings about absolute surrender in His power, in His timing and in His own way. Personally, I have had several mile markers along the way, events that have stopped me in my tracks and have challenged me, yet again, to surrender more.

We read in Philippians 2:13, "It is God that works in you both to will and to do of His good pleasure." He desires to work in us and to accomplish His perfect will, but this requires an absolute surrender of our will in exchange for His. If this exchange does not take place in our lives, we will forever be stunted and hindered from all that the Lord has for us.

Abraham was unfaithful and disobedient on his own but God worked in Him, raising him up and preparing him to take the role of the father of many nations. God made Abraham an instrument of His glory. This took place over time as Abraham learned to know and trust God. It blesses me that God put the story of Abraham and Sarah in the Bible to show us that no one is perfect and the process of complete surrender truly happens over a lifetime.

Though I surrendered my life to Jesus in 1987, since then I have experienced many years of yielding to God. As with Abraham and Sarah, that there were certain monumental events, I like to think of them as mile markers along the way— that spurred on my continual surrender.

My first mile marker was that Tuesday in 1987 when I went forward at Calvary Chapel Costa Mesa and rededicated my life to the Lord (for the third time). But, this time it stuck. I really meant it. Slowly but surely, I began to see some fruit in my life as I chose to abide in the True Vine, Jesus. Surrender and obedience go hand in hand. At nineteen years old, I was finished trying to do it my way and was ready to let Him have His way in my life. For the next five years, I would be in a steady process of surrender, sometimes obeying and experiencing victory and growth, and other times giving in, giving up and giving over to my flesh instead of to the Holy Spirit, therefore hindering the work that the Lord desired to accomplish in me.

At twenty-four, another mile marker exchange occurred when I met my husband. It as though the Lord was saying, "Here is a great opportunity for you, one that I have hand delivered." I didn't see it coming, but because I was abiding and obeying, the Lord allowed me to recognize that my intended husband was indeed from Him. When we choose the will of the Lord over our own wills, His plans become crystal clear. Oh, His plan may look very different than we imagined, but His plan for us is so much better than what we can imagine.

At twenty-nine, I experienced yet another mile marker of surrender when we moved our family to Florida to plant Calvary Chapel Brandon. This was an exciting time in our lives, a time of trusting the Lord for every penny and every morsel of food. It was a time of plowing and planting, a time of tears of sorrow and tears of joy, and a time of personal growth and church growth. As we stepped out in faith we were stretched and encouraged as we saw the Lord work miracles. We moved with no job and zero savings. We met for church in a living room, coffee house, recreation center, strip mall, and furniture store before finally purchasing our own building, a former Baptist Church. Soon, we acquired a radio station and started a school. My mother- and father-in-law joined us by moving to Florida to help us with the church. God was good, He was blessing, and we were in for the long haul. We loved and spiritually fed our sweet church body faithfully for ten years and were happy to remain in Florida for the rest of our lives . . . but God had a different plan.

But God—these two three-letter words that mean so much. We see these words used in the Scriptures and often pass over them. But let's camp on them for a moment:

But God remembered Noah and all the wild animals and the livestock that were with him in the ark, and he sent a wind over the earth, and the waters receded (Genesis 8:1 NIV, emphasis added).

You intended to harm me, *but God* intended it for good to accomplish what is now being done, the saving of many lives (Genesis 50:20 NIV, emphasis added).

David stayed in the wilderness strongholds and in the hills of the Desert of Ziph. Day after day Saul searched for him, *but God* did not give David into his hands (1 Samuel 23:14 NIV, emphasis added).

But now the Lord my *God* has given me rest on every side, and there is no adversary or disaster (1 Kings 5:4 NIV, emphasis added).

But God will redeem me from the realm of the dead; He will surely take me to himself (Psalm 49:15 NIV, emphasis added).

God is the one who leads and guides us. He protects us, and even uses for good in our lives what the enemy has intended for evil. He gives us rest from our enemies and He alone sees the big picture, when we see only in part. Sometimes we think we know the mind of the Lord, and then we're thrown a curve ball, something that is not as we planned. But we have to learn to factor God into our equations, trusting that His plans are bigger and better than we could ever expect.

Our curve ball was thrown in 2006. We had been happily serving the Lord in Florida for ten years and were content to spend the rest of our lives there—until the Lord began loosening our hold. He began to reveal His continued will for our lives, which was to move back to Southern California (something we said we would never do). What began as an inkling quickly developed into a possibility, and over the course of three months, it became a reality. Through much confirmation, we took the step to put our house on the market and it sold a month later. I remember having a conversation with my husband about how crazy this was, and he shared with me that the Lord told him that He could send anyone, but He was sending us! The question then became, would we obey?

As with anything the Lord asks of us, we have a choice whether to obey or not. Why would we leave our home, our family, and our precious church that we birthed to move back to a place we said we'd never go back to? Because God asked— and we obeyed.

It's so hard to understand God's ways when you're in the moment. We don't see as He sees; we aren't omniscient. This is where faith comes in. Hebrew 11:1 says, "Faith is the substance of things hoped for and the evidence of things unseen." Faith is also revealed through the Word of God: Faith comes by hearing and hearing by the Word of God (Romans 10:17).

As we diligently sought God for direction, He revealed His will and His plan for our lives, which was very different from ours. We thought Florida was our resting place, but He saw it as our training ground. In Florida we learned to work hard and to trust the Lord for little things like food and bigger things like buildings. We saw the Lord do miracles and change lives. We watched kids grow up, get married and start families. We learned what prayer really meant and the importance of prayer in the church. We enjoyed the body of Christ and loved our southern friends. *But God* began stirring and speaking to our hearts so much so that we would be disobedient not to respond to His call. This call would come at a high cost as we were ripped from family and friends, our church and all our kids knew as home to start over—not by choice but by obedience.

Oswald Chambers describes the great exchange of our wills for His like an island in the ocean. You can see the top, but in reality it's much bigger and much deeper than the eye can see. As we give up our rights to ourselves and hand them over to God, Jesus will emancipate us by transforming us into His image. The more rights we surrender to Him, the more we become like Him. His desire is that we are one with Him. Jesus describes this process in John 15:1-4:

"I am the true vine, and My Father is the vinedresser. Every branch in Me that does not bear fruit He takes away; and every branch that bears fruit He prunes, that it may bear more fruit. You are already clean because of the word which I have spoken to you. Abide in Me, and I in you. As the branch cannot bear fruit of itself, unless it abides in the vine, neither can you, unless you abide in Me."

The process of abiding in Jesus is deeper and wider than we can see, but in the end we're solid, strong and immovable. As our will is laid down and His is picked up, our lives take on new depths, new character, new meaning . . . our lives become His, our desires become His, and our wills becomes His. It's impossible to explain how this happens, but from personal experience I know when we become less He becomes more. As we yield, abide and obey, we enter into His perfect will for our lives. The results are astonishing as our lives become less and less about us and more and more about Him. When we are living, dwelling, and remaining connected to the Vine, surrender is much easier.

My journey of surrender didn't stop when we moved back to California. In fact, the move picked up the pace. I experienced one of my biggest and longest mile markers in 2007. This lesson would take five months to learn. Moreover, it was such a great lesson that I have dedicated the next chapter to it.

4

Tapped Out!

~ learning to be humble ~

At times we need to hit rock bottom, even as believers, before we will listen to what the Lord is trying to say to us. We often unknowingly wrestle with God as Jacob did in Genesis 32. Many years after stealing his brother's birthright and lying to his father, Isaac, Jacob found himself desiring reconciliation with his estranged family. We read in Genesis 32 how Jacob arranged to finally meet up with Esau on the other side of the ford of the Jabbok. Jacob sent his whole family across the brook and he stayed alone on the other side, wrestling with God all night.

Have you ever felt that way? That everyone else has passed over to the other side except you . . . that you are holding on to something that hinders you from crossing over? Maybe you find yourself doing mental gymnastics, retracing your steps, trying to figure out how things will work out . . . while the Lord sits waiting for you to tap out and give up. That sounds contradictory, doesn't it? *Give up?* We are taught to *press on, persevere* and *endure.* But when it comes to wrestling with God, we will always lose.

When we read that Jacob wrestled with God all night and wouldn't let go (see Gen. 32:22-32), there's a tendency to think that Jacob was defending himself, which he was. But Jacob's struggle with the Lord was not self-defense; this was mental defense. Jacob thought he was justified to feel the way he did—justified to steal the birthright because his brother, Esau, really wasn't taking it seriously. Therefore, Jacob cheated his brother Esau from what was rightfully his. During Jacob's wrestling match with the Lord, we read that God touched and dislocated Jacob's hip. This demonstrates to us that God could have easily defeated Jacob at anytime. The lesson for Jacob was humility. He had to be humbled to become humble. Compared to God, Jacob was nothing.

Even though Jacob fought with God, we see that he does something brave and remarkable: he refused to give up until God gave him a blessing. You see, everything changed after Jacob was touched by God. He continued to wrestle, but now it was *for* God, not *against* God. I believe the reason for his encounter with God was to ensure that Jacob, who became Israel, had the correct motivation, the right heart, and a humble attitude toward God. Jacob responded to the lesson in humility by a show of faith and longing for God.

Like Jacob we, too, can wrestle with God—not physically but spiritually. I did this for five long months, and it was exhausting. It felt like a physical wrestling match. The problem, though, was that I didn't realize *who* I was wrestling with and *why* I was even wrestling. Jesus is so longsuffering and kind that He allows us time to repent and turn from our sin; however, the length of our wrestling match is often determined by us. It took me five months to get my eyes off myself and onto Him. Jesus allowed me to go until I couldn't go any longer, and when I was finally ready to listen to Him, He touched me. It was a beautiful thing. I was like JELL-O in His hands. As I wept and asked for His forgiveness, our fellowship was immediately restored.

You see, all along it was me. *I* was the one who was hindering God's voice from being heard. All my anger and bitterness stood in the way. Once I was alone with the Lord and began putting all of that aside to truly seek Him, He touched me—not physically but spiritually. God touched my heart, and I heard Him speak sweet words with a tender voice of love and not one of rebuke: "Michelle, the problem is you. You are not content with what I have given you . . . it's *Me* that you are fighting and no one else. This is My doing."

Wow! I had no idea that it was the Lord whom I was upset with. He had blessed me, and I was complaining about His provision. Like Jacob, it took God's touching me and humbling me to reveal my heart.

You see, we moved back from Florida to Southern California after a ten-year absence. We had gotten to the place in our lives that we were comfortable. We had moved three times while in Florida, each time purchasing a larger home for our growing family. We had gone from A to B to C, and we were now at D. And D was a good place to be! But the Lord called us back to Southern California, and we thought we wouldn't be able to afford to buy a home. My fear was that we would go back to A—and that we did! The Lord was asking me to trust Him and I was in fear.

While my husband was in California at a conference, I had only a few small requests for him as he went house hunting. My main request: a four-bedroom home with a decent kitchen. Not too much to ask, right? Apparently, it was too much because what he rented was a box on top of a box—a three-bedroom place with a square for a kitchen. They called it a house, but we were so close to our neighbors that when I heard their phone ringing, I answered ours! I can laugh about it now, but I assure you, I wasn't laughing then.

We managed to squeeze our family of six into that little home. The one and only plus to this house was that it had a beautiful ocean view. Unfortunately, I didn't appreciate the view for the first five months, until I tapped out, gave up and surrendered to the Lord. Then, I looked out at our backyard and for the first time thanked the Lord for His provision, His plan, and His loving kindness that drew me to repentance. It would be two years of living in that home before the Lord would move us on.

Our God is so good to us, especially when we don't deserve it. On Valentines Day, just to show me how very much He loves me, despite my unfaithfulness to Him, Jesus blessed us with buying a beautiful home that exceeded any of my expectations, let alone my requests. I even had the opportunity to pray with our landlord to receive Jesus into her heart before we moved. As Ephesians 3:20 tells us, "[He] is able to do exceedingly abundantly above all that we ask or think."

I wish I could say that I have never wrestled with God again. I have, but now that I've learned the valuable lesson in humility and surrender, I tap out much earlier. I also learned to look for God's hand in all things—good and bad. I see Him orchestrating all things for my good in my life, and recognize they are His doing.

Are you at a place in your walk that you, like Jacob, are wrestling with God? Do both yourself and me a favor and let Him have his way. Tap out, and listen to what He would say to you. Many of us admire Jacob for his tenacity, in not giving up the fight, when in actuality, he was being stubborn and had to be physically afflicted and humbled to let go of the clinging.

Are you clinging to something too tightly because you won't give it up to serve God? He loves you so much that He will let you cling for a while, and then He will touch you. Sometimes He will do so to correct us and other times He will do so to melt us. Open your eyes today to the things that are His doing. Are you in financial trouble? It could be His doing. Are you being tested in patience with the people around you? It could be His doing. Are you experiencing a time of sorrow? It could be His doing. Has He taken you back from D to A? It could be His doing. God places us in the perfect school to learn the lessons that He wants as to learn to make us more like Him.

For My thoughts *are* not your thoughts, Nor *are* your ways My ways," says the Lord. "For *as* the heavens are higher than the earth, So are My ways higher than your ways, And My thoughts than your thoughts (Isaiah 55:8-9).

Don't forget to factor in His school of humility when trying to figure out or fix things on your own. He loves us so very much that He always works all things together for good in our lives to accomplish His perfect will. Remember, His doings in your life ultimately bring out the best in you. So tap out, humble yourself and let Him have His way. He loves you so very much!

5

My Father, the Gardener

~ learning to thank Him for the thorns ~

Coming to the realization as a new believer that you are *not* in control anymore is both wonderful and scary all at the same time. It seems that this process never ends and that we are continually being molded into His image the longer we walk with Him.

Paul describes it as looking into a mirror made of tarnished silver and seeing his reflection only dimly. One day, Paul says, we will see clearly, face-to-face. But, until then, the Lord is changing us into the very image of Jesus. The longer we walk with the Lord, drawing nearer to Him, obeying Him, and spending more time with Him, we will naturally take on His likeness. As we grow in the Lord, we, like fruit trees, will need to be cut back, or pruned to bear more fruit. Because our Heavenly Father loves us, He takes care to cut away anything that may hinder our growth.

John 15 tells us He is the vine and we are the branches. He is the Vinedresser who takes care of His crop. He waters, fertilizes, and yes, cuts off what will no longer produce fruit so that we may bear even more fruit. This can be a painful process in a believer's life, and one that can either be received or rejected.   As our Heavenly Gardener, the Lord certainly knows what to trim and what to leave. He is in control of the pruning. Even though this can be hard, uncomfortable, difficult, and downright painful, we must trust that the Lord knows what He's doing. We must yield to His pruning process, knowing that His fruit is greater than the pain of the pruning.

L.B. Cowman said, "Many of the richest blessings we have inherited are the fruit of sorrow or pain. We should never forget that redemption, the world's greatest blessing, is the fruit of the world's greatest sorrow. And whenever a time of deep pruning comes and the knife cuts deeply and the pain is severe, what an inexpressible comfort it is to know: 'My Father is the gardener.'"[i]

We should never forget that redemption, the world's greatest blessing, is the fruit of the world's greatest sorrow.

I don't know very much about roses, but I do know that in California, they need to be cut back at the beginning of the year to bloom in the spring. When we moved to our new home, I was excited to have rose bushes, although I wasn't sure how to take care of them. The first year, I cut just the buds off, and not many flowers came back. The next year, I was told that you have to cut everything off the bush: buds, leaves and branches, leaving only the stub. My roses looked ugly and even sad, but in a few months new healthy leaves and fresh blooms appeared—even more than the year before.

While trimming those rose bushes I thought of my life and how necessary it is for the Lord to rid me of certain things that may hinder my growth in Him. I realized that though pruning is painful at times, it's necessary in order to bear more fruit each year. I also realized that pruning is just as necessary as planting. In fact, it's in the pruning stage that I've personally grown the most in my walk with the Lord. I've learned to appreciate the process, even though I cannot say that I enjoy it.

John Vincent, a Methodist Episcopal bishop of the late nineteenth and early twentieth century, once told of himself in a large greenhouse where clusters of luscious grapes were hanging on each side. The owner of the greenhouse told him, "When the new gardener came here, he said he would not work with the vines unless he could cut them completely down to the stalk. I allowed him to do so, and we had no grapes for two years, but this is now the result.[ii]

Notice that the gardener had to cut back the grapevine to nothing—no life left, just a naked stem. Likewise, we too have times of being cut back severely to the point of feeling completely bare. As the Heavenly Gardener prunes us, it seems as though He is destroying our vine, cutting away any and all life. Yet, He sees the end result. He sees what we cannot see. He sees all the fruit stemming forth from a beautiful, healthy plant. All we feel is the pain, loneliness and heartache, but He sees the abundant fruit spilling forth from a healthy life with Christ.

There are many blessings we will never receive until we are ready to pay the price of pain, because suffering often is the way to reach them. I think this little poem by J.R. Miller sums it up beautifully:

I walked a mile with Pleasure;
She chattered all the way,
But left me none the wiser
For all she had to say
I walked a mile with Sorrow,
And not a word said she;
But oh, the things I learned from her
When Sorrow walked with me![iii]

Charles Spurgeon said about sorrow, "How would you like to stand there [in heaven] and be pointed out as the only saint who never experienced sorrow? Never! You would feel like a stranger in the midst of a sacred fellowship. Therefore, may we be content to share in the battle, for we will soon wear a crown of reward and wave a palm branch of praise."[iv]

Paul the apostle knew well about suffering, sorrow, pain and praise. In 2 Corinthians 12:10 he said, "For Christ's sake I delight in weakness, in insults, in hardships, in persecutions, in difficulties. For when I am weak, then I am strong" (NIV). To delight in weakness means to *take pleasure* in your weaknesses, for when you are without strength, that is when you are strong. In Greek, this strength is expressed as *dunamis,* meaning "dynamite power" or "dynamic."

Can we say what Paul says, that we take pleasure in our weakness, in being without strength, in being insulted? Do we really believe that when we are weak and powerless, when we are without strength, that is when we are truly the most powerful? That is when He comes in, and through His Spirit, makes us dynamite! It is when we come to the end of ourselves that Jesus becomes all we need. We stop seeking sympathy from others for our difficulties and ill treatment, and we realize that pruning is indeed necessary for our growth.

Paul said in Romans 8:28, "And we *know* that all things work together for the good of those who love God and are the called according to His purpose" (emphasis added). *All things*—not just some, but all, of our circumstances in life as Believers are allowed by the Lord for our continued growth in Him. George Matheson, a blind preacher from Scotland, once said, "My dear God, I have never thanked You for my thorns. I have thanked You a thousand times for my roses but not once for my thorns."

How true. We thank the Lord for our blessings and neglect to see the value and purpose of the thorns. The thorns are just as beneficial as the rosebuds, because without the thorns we wouldn't have rose blooms. You see, the thorns protect the roses from predators. The same is true with us. Believe it or not, the thorns are actually helping us to stay alive, vibrant and attractive. So, if you are being persecuted, treated unkindly, or experiencing difficulties and hardships, try thanking the Lord, knowing that He is using those thorns to make you into a beautiful rose.

I recently learned that the world's supply of rose oil comes from the Balkan Mountains. The interesting thing is that these roses are gathered during the darkest hours, between 1:00and 2:00 a.m. Scientific tests have proven that 40 percent of the fragrance of those roses disappeared in the light of day. So, too, with believers. Our character is strengthened most in the darkest days. That's when our fragrance for Christ is the most potent.

Jesus said in John 15:2, "Every branch in me that does not bear fruit he takes away, and every branch that does bear fruit he prunes, that it may bear more fruit."

Regarding this statement of Jesus, Charles Spurgeon said:

This is a precious promise to the one who lives to be fruitful. At first it seems to wear a sharp aspect. Must the fruitful bough be pruned? Must the knife cut even the best and most useful? There's no doubt about it, for much of our Lord's purging work is done by means of afflictions of one kind or another. It is not the evil but the good who have the promise of tribulation in this life. But, then, the end more than makes up for the painful nature of the means. If we can bring forth more fruit for our Lord, we will not mind the pruning and the loss of our foliage.[v]

If you're in the midst of a time of pruning, be encouraged that you will soon bloom and become even more fruitful than before. The Lord sees and knows your pain and has a plan for everything He does!

For I know the thoughts that I think toward you, says the Lord, thoughts of peace and not of evil, to give you a future and a hope (Jeremiah 29:11).

6

Great Faith Tested

~ learning to believe ~

On several occasions in my life, I have exercised what I would consider *great faith*. I think of our move to Florida to plant Calvary Chapel Brandon, not having a place to live or a job, and not knowing what we would do, or whether the church plant would even work. During that time we had twelve envelopes, each containing the exact amount of cash for our rent, marked with the month, but with no money allotted for food.

It amazed us that people actually showed up to our church services. We didn't have a website, flyers or posters and of course, no smartphones, Facebook pages or Instagram accounts—just a couple of A-frame signs sitting outside the recreation center. Though we were without technology, we had the joy and privilege of watching God bring people to the church the good old-fashioned way—by word of mouth.

Some heard about the church, others happened upon the church, yet others saw the signs. It really was a complete miracle that anyone came. Also, miraculous were our many ventures of faith while in Florida: purchasing homes, buildings, a radio station and starting a school. But none seems to compare to the lesson the Lord taught me in faith when our daughter was born. It seems that once the Lord has given us great faith, He will test that faith with long delays.

It's funny how we tend to have great faith for others but seem to be of little faith when it comes to our own lives. Jesus never said that our faith had to be big; in fact, He said it could be very small. In Matthew 17:20 Jesus shares how little faith can do big things: "I say to you, if you have faith as a mustard seed, you will say to this mountain, 'Move from here to there,' and it will move; and nothing will be impossible for you." This was a great lesson that I had yet to learn.

Somehow, I was able to have big faith for the church, but when it came to personal matters my faith shrunk. I trusted Him for many things as we sojourned in Florida, but there was one thing I thought He may have overlooked. I was so blessed by my three sons, but I really had a desire for a little girl. My heart longed to dress her up, paint her nails, giggle together, have tea parties and of course shop together. I would go to baby showers of little girls and long to have a pink room with white accents and flowers. I found myself struggling to rejoice with

"Delight yourself in the Lord and He will give you the desires of your heart" Psalm 37:4.

my friends who were expecting baby girls. So, I went to God's Word and came across Psalm 37:4: "Delight yourself in the Lord and He will give you the desires of your heart." As I read on, I was blessed . . . verse 5: *"Commit* your way to the Lord, *trust* also in Him and He will bring it to pass" (emphasis added). *Delight, commit, trust*—easier said then done, but I was determined to do those three things and hold firmly to the promises of my Jesus, knowing that He indeed had planted those desires in my heart long ago and that He would bring them to pass.

Several years passed and my longing for a little girl only grew stronger. One night, while I was praying with one of our sons, who was six at the time, he asked Jesus for a little sister. I was surprised to hear this from him as I never shared my desire for a little girl with my boys. Every night for six months, he prayed the same fervent prayer, and the Lord heard and answered this sweet boy. When I became pregnant, deep down I knew the Lord indeed had answered the simple childlike prayer of a six-year-old boy.

Waiting for nineteen weeks seemed an eternity. While on vacation I wrote in my journal about my fear of having another boy. I think I was most fearful to disappoint our son and risk him feeling as though the Lord hadn't answered his heartfelt and confident prayers. I wrestled while on vacation, reading, writing and listening to the Lord speak. I was so disappointed in myself for not believing when my little boy remained so confident that the Lord had heard and answered his prayer. My constant prayer was, *Lord, help my unbelief.* It boggled my mind how I could trust the Lord to provide food when there was no money, and to open church buildings when there was no where to go, yet find it so difficult to trust Him to give me my heart's desire. I found comfort in the Scriptures, knowing that I was delighting in Him. I had committed my ways to Him, and I did truly trust in Him. Therefore, He would definitely give me my heart's desires.

On August 19, 2003, we went for our ultrasound, and the Lord brought His will to pass in our lives as we saw Him answer my unspoken prayer and the childlike, fervent, confident prayer of a six-year-old boy. Yes, He truly grants us the desires of our hearts if we are delighting in Him, committed to Him, and trusting in Him. He will bring it to pass. Ironically, my due date was Valentine's Day, which was yet another sweet reminder that He does give us the desires of our hearts. We named her Faith Abigail, not because of my great faith, but because of the faith of our six-year-old son! Since then, I have been able to encourage many women with these words knowing, that the Lord has planted our desires in our hearts long before He brings them to pass.

We read in Genesis about Abraham, who desired to have a child and was even promised a child by the Lord long before there was any indication of its fulfillment. Abraham called himself a father before he was a father because God called him "the father of many nations" (Genesis 17:4). Abraham lived by faith and believed God by faith. He took God at His word. He stepped out on thin air and found solid rock beneath his feet.

When a young bird first learns to fly, the fledgling flits into the air hoping its little wings will keep them from falling. At first, the bird may fear falling despite wings for support. But, if its wings fail, a parent will swoop down and retrieve the youngling to safety. Jesus rescues us in the same way. At times

He nudges us from our nest to step out in faith but if we are not ready to fly He is right there to catch us. He tells us, "Fear not for I am with you; do not be dismayed, for I am your God. I will strengthen you, yes, I will help you, I will uphold you with My righteous right hand" (Isaiah 41:10).

We have nothing to fear, for our God is with us. He sees us and knows us. He knows our lying down and our waking. He knows our thoughts before we even think them (see Psalm 139). If God knows us this intimately, surely we can trust Him . . . right? Thinking back to Abraham and Sarah, we know that although they trusted God, they did waver at one point, taking it upon themselves to help God out. This godly couple filled with great faith, was tested and they failed. Had they waited a little longer they would have seen God come through as He said. But, they grew impatient with waiting. This is where we tend to go wrong. If we read on in Psalm 37, after we delight, commit, and trust our ways to the Lord, we are then to wait: "Be still before the Lord and wait patiently for Him" (verse 7 NLT).

We tend to do good waiting for a while and then we grow weary waiting and we move forward without God, much like Abraham and Sarah taking it upon themselves to bring forth the promised child in the flesh, while all along God had something of the Spirit waiting to be fulfilled. I'm so very blessed that this story is in the Bible, because we so often move ahead of the Lord, not seeing unanswered prayers as delays but as refusals. We move forward, making mistakes and jumping ahead of the Lord, and then have to go back and repent and try to repair our mistakes, if they are even repairable. Sarah offered her maidservant Hagar to Abraham in an effort to help God out. This made things worse and resulted in division, bitterness, hatred and envy. When we read of Ishmael in the Scriptures, he always refers a type of the flesh. Bitterness, anger, hatred, division and envy are all of the flesh.

The great lesson for us is not to interfere with the Lord's timing, no matter how hard it is to wait, knowing that His timing is always perfect. When you are tempted to rush things a bit, remember Ishmael. Nothing good will result when we try to help God out. He works on His own timeline in His own timeframe, which is always perfectly blessed!

Ishmael was just the beginning for Abraham. God increased Abraham's faith with each step he took, ultimately leading to the biggest step of faith he would ever take: offering up his son Isaac in obedience to God. The person whose faith has been severely tested, yet comes through victorious, is the person who will experience even greater tests to come. This not only strengthens our faith, but it increases our testimony to others as well. When Abraham offered his son up on Mount Moriah, I'm sure he had no idea how many lives would later be affected by his act of obedience.

We read this story in awe and amazement, thinking, *I could never do that!* But, we fail to realize that Isaac was the object of Abraham's great love. And although we may not physically walk up a mountain and build an altar and use rope to tie down our sacrifice, we are still called, just like Abraham was, to lay down things or people or possessions, sacrificing them to God as an act of obedience. This act proved to God that nothing, not even Abraham's greatest possession on earth, was more important than obeying God. God wants our affections and will often will put our faith to the test to see where we stand. Are we faithful to Him? Do we trust Him?

Elijah is another man who had his great faith tested. He stood up to the four hundred prophets of Baal and trusted God to show up on his behalf, and He did. He killed all four hundred false prophets and had a mighty victory, yet he ran for his life because of threats from wicked Queen Jezebel. Elijah trusted God for the big things but wavered in the small things: protection, provision and people. Just like Abraham and Sarah, Elijah trusted God for what He could do through him, but wavered in trusting for what He would do for him. Elijah saw the hand of God just like Abraham and Sarah, but it was after a time of doubt and despair. The Lord showed up when Elijah was on the run and provided meat and water at the Broke Cherith. The Lord commanded Elijah in 1 Kings 17:3-4 to go and hide himself by the Brook Cherith, and there the Lord would provide him with food, water, shelter and fellowship with God Himself.

There are times in our lives, often after a great victory, like Elijah's, when we are in need of secluded time alone with the Lord. Whether our faith is being tested or we are in need of direction, protection, or just connection, getting alone with God in a still, quiet, peaceful place is a must if we want to hear from Him. We live in a very fast-paced world. We are always in a hurry and moving quickly here and there. We want things fast and are constantly on a schedule. This isn't always bad if we are using our time wisely, but as with Elijah, there are times we need to go hide away at the Brook Cherith, and let the Lord minister to us: *Let Me fill you up and nourish your soul.* Where is your peaceful place of solitude? Where is your Brook Cherith, the place where you have quiet communion with God, the place where you find refuge, even for a moment, the place where you are lost in His presence? Run to that place and be still before Him.

Our lives must be quiet and peaceful if we want to see God. When we get a glimpse of God, our lives are forever changed. As one commentator said, "Every saintly soul that would wield great power with men must win it in some hidden A Carmel triumph always presupposes a Cherith; and a Cherith always leads to a Carmel."[vi]

The best example we have of this in scripture is Jesus Himself, who found it necessary to spend time alone in solitude before God. None of us is exempt from a Brook Cherith experience, where the sounds of human voices are exchanged for the waters of quietness that flow from the throne of God. Go to the Brook, taste the sweetness of the Lord, and soak up His power . . . knowing that the testing of your faith produces patience. Allow God to have His way with you. Allow Him to accomplish His perfect plan for you, and trust Him to grant you your heart's desires. Delight in Him, commit your ways to Him, and trust Him to bring His perfect plan to pass as you wait and do not fret.

Abraham didn't grow in his faith by giant leaps but by one step of faith at a time, and we can do the same. God knows when to withhold something from us and when to grant it. His timing is perfect! Someone once said God's delays are not His refusals. Many prayers are received and recorded, yet underneath are the words, "My time has not yet come." Be patient with God's timing!

7

Discipline, the Hard Surrender

~ learning to make it my career ~

I have discovered that it truly takes discipline to put Jesus first. Elizabeth Elliot in her book *Discipline the Glad Surrender* explains that as a child in a Christian home, she "did not start out with an understanding of the word *discipline.*" She said, "I simply knew that I belonged to people that loved me and cared for me. That is dependence. They spoke to me and I answered. That is responsibility. They gave me things to do and I did them. That is obedience. It adds up to discipline. In other words, the totality of the believer's response [to dependence, responsibility and obedience] is discipline."[vii]

Discipline and obedience go hand in hand. Discipline defines and shapes our lives as believers, while obedience refers to a specific action. We need both to be disciples of the Lord. Obedience is the first step to becoming disciplined.

God blessed Adam and Eve and gave them responsibility in the Garden to be fruitful and multiply. God revealed to Noah His plan to destroy the earth and told Noah that he and his family would escape if they obeyed. Abraham was chosen to be "the father of many nations," but strict obedience was required of Abraham, and a life of faith and sacrifice would follow. Moses heard the voice of God in the burning bush and responded in obedience. Samuel, David, Jeremiah, Matthew and Paul the apostle acted in obedience to the call of God upon their lives.

These men weren't concerned about being well-known, successful or even great in God's kingdom. They were only concerned about fulfilling the will of God in their lives. "Discipline," says Elizabeth Elliot, "is the believer's answer to God's call."[viii] Discipline is the recognition of God's master plan for our lives and we can take it or leave it—it's up to us.

"Discipline is the believer's answer to God's call."

Discipline has been called "the Disciples Career." We are constantly trying to become more disciplined in our quiet time, in prayer, diet, exercise, studies or whatever it is to us (you fill in the blank). At times, it seems we are going around in circles with discipline. Sometimes we have it and other times we don't. We look at men like George Mueller, George Whitfield and R. C. Chapman and wonder if we could ever have the discipline to go to bed by 10:00 p.m. and get up at 4:00 a.m. every morning.

Lest we be too hard on ourselves, it appears as though we have it much harder then those men in only one way:

technology: TV, smart phones, tablets, computers, social media like Facebook and Instagram, Snapchat and Twitter, to name a few, all vying for our constant attention. It's so difficult to be as disciplined as we'd like to be because we are so easily distracted. We read of these men and women of old and say, "That was then and this is now."

But what we fail to see is that these men and women of yesteryear had power, and we lack power. They had focus and we lack focus. They had discipline, and we lack discipline. Jesus said those who want to follow Him must leave self behind, take up their cross, and follow Him. In leaving ourselves behind, we often find out where our hearts truly lie. Are we for Him or against Him? Do we love Him, or are we just fond of Him?

While in college, Elizabeth Elliott hoped to get Jim Elliott to write sweet endearing words in her yearbook. What he wrote she never forgot: "A Soldier on active service will not let himself be involved in civilian affairs, he must be wholly at his commanding officers disposal." Elizabeth understood his quote from 2 Timothy 2:4 loud and clear. Jim's life was wholly surrendered to the Lord, and if the two of them had a future together, it would have to be revealed by his commanding officer, Jesus Christ.[ix]

We, too, are soldiers enlisted in the battle and we must be mindful that nothing gets in the way of hearing from our commanding officer. Discipline for the Christian begins with the body. It's what we are called to sacrifice. We present, offer and give our bodies continually to the Lord for His purposes. This is our reasonable service. This is our act of worship. Surrendering our bodies is the starting place. Failure here means failure everywhere else.

Jesus said we are to "deny [ourselves], take up [our] cross daily, and follow [Him]" (Luke 9:23). This is no easy task. In fact the act of dying to self is a daily task, one of which I'm slowly learning.

Some time ago, my husband and I went to serve at an outreach out of state. We got in late at night and finally made it to our hotel. I had just finished sharing with him about the book I had been reading on the plane, *Discipline: The Glad Surrender*. I had just finished the chapter in which Elizabeth shared about the two main qualities needed in ministry: flexibility and humility. As we got to our room we were both tired and hungry, but we decided to go right to sleep. As I pulled back the covers on the bed, there to greet me was a big cockroach . . . alive! my husband laughed because of what I just shared with him about humility and flexibility. But I didn't laugh. I was tired, and hungry and disgusted. But I knew God was working on me, so I got right into bed after the cockroach crawled away, hoping its family wasn't in bed with me.

The next day, the air conditioning went out in the hotel when it was 95 degrees outside. It was my turn to remind my husband of the need for flexibility and humility and this time I was the one who laughed. But he didn't think it was funny. At this point, we started to think that the Lord was trying to tell us something, so we listened as the Lord gave us a crash course in flexibility and humility. This crash course would continue and still is continuing to this day.

When struggling in this area, I often lean on the words of Pastor Chuck Smith (founder of Calvary Chapel): "Blessed are the flexible for they shall not be broken." Oh, how these words have been a source of comfort and strength in due season. I am learning slowly but surely that humility precedes flexibility. To be humble is to not think of oneself too highly. In fact, it really is to not think of oneself at all. We need to be emptied of *self* to be useful to the Kingdom of God. My husband has added to Pastor Chuck's words with, "Blessed are the flexible, for they shall not be broken—but they will be stretched!"

Paul the apostle knew this well and serves as a great example to us of one who matured in humility over time. We see the five-year progression that begins in 1 Corinthians 15:9, where Paul said, "I am the least of the apostles." Four years later he said he was, "less than the least of all the saints" (Ephesians 3:8); and finally a year after that, Paul announced that he was the chief of sinners (see 1 Timothy 1:15). That's humility and maturity. Paul learned quickly, but it took his being humbled to do it.

It's been said that you will either be humble or humbled. If you remain humble, you will be usable. The key to humility can be found in John 3:30, where John the Baptist said of Jesus, "He must increase, but I must decrease." Along that line Augustine said, "Do you wish to rise? Begin by descending. You plan a tower that will pierce the clouds? Lay first the foundation of humility."

Humility, flexibility and obedience hinge on a disciplined life. It's when we put Jesus first, daily, and allow Him to increase in our lives that we begin to decrease. It's when we slowly learn over time the blessings of not thinking of ourselves at all, but instead allow Jesus to take over and take all of us. The Key to the disciplined life is indeed a fully surrendered life. As we learn to surrender all of ourselves, we will become flexible, humble and obedient.

Is it easy? Absolutely not! Is it necessary? Absolutely! He makes all things beautiful in His time. Allow Him room to work! And remember—discipline and obedience go hand-in-hand.

8

The Balancing Act

~ learning not to be overtaken ~

Jesus announced to His disciples in Matthew 16:24-25, "If anyone desires to come after Me, let him deny himself, and take up his cross, and follow Me. For whoever desires to save his life will lose it, but whoever loses his life for My sake will find it."

Jesus calls us to sacrifice our body to Him, to die to our selfish desires, and to crucify the flesh. We can't give our hearts to the Lord and keep our bodies for ourselves. The bodies of believers are where the Holy Spirit dwells, which house the heart, mind, will and emotions. We must keep our bodies healthy but never allow that pursuit to take priority over our relationship with the Lord. There is balance in life, and we, as Believers, must learn this.

Paul said in Galatians 2:20, "I have been crucified with Christ; it is no longer I who live, but Christ who lives in me; and the life which I now live in the flesh I live by faith in the Son of God, who loved me and gave himself for me."

Realizing this changes everything. If I have truly died to myself (crucified with Christ) then my old woman is dead and needs never to be resurrected again. All of the things I used to do before I was saved now must first be filtered through my Father in Heaven. Who I was before is now dead, and I'm a new creature in Christ. But this is easier said than done, isn't it?

The longer you sow to the flesh, the harder this truth becomes. Although saved at 19, I did some serious damage that could not be reversed. I had sown to my flesh just long enough to have life long consequences, and the side effects would take some time to undo. I read and reread Psalm 103:12: "As far as the east is from the west, so far has He removed our transgressions from us." Trusting that God cannot lie and that my sins were indeed forgiven, I embraced this Scripture verse and other verses that spoke of God's great love and forgiveness toward me. As I received these promises and began to obey the word, bit by bit I was able to see that I was imbalanced in almost every area of my life.

Balance is defined as "an even distribution of weight, enabling someone or something to remain upright and steady," and "a situation in which different elements are equal or in the correct proportions."[x] This balancing act has been a tough one for me to conquer. I've never had very much balance in my life. I grew up training for gymnastics six hours a day, six days a week. This instilled in me a great work ethic but an imbalance in my life—one that would take years for me to fully surrender over to the Lord.

Balance is an area that is difficult for most people. We tend to be either overachievers or underachievers, those who don't rest until it's finished—a perfectionist, or those who wait and procrastinate. I have been both, and don't like either of them. Jesus said, "I have come that they may have life, and that they may have it more abundantly" (John 10:10). Jesus desires a full, rich and balanced life for His followers.

I have always considered myself a very disciplined person. I was trained at an early age that "practice makes perfect," and always worked hard and did my best at sports and in school. I learned to never give up and became tenacious in everything, but to my detriment I became excessive in most things. Instead of a one-day fast, I would fast for a week. Instead of running three miles, I would run ten. Instead of drinking a quart of water, I'd drink a gallon. This became my life. I was proud to be disciplined in eating right and exercise, but I allowed it to overcome me, and soon it overtook me. Diet and exercise became my gods. I disciplined my body but failed to discipline my mind. I allowed myself to be conformed to the world and its way of thinking.

For many years, I struggled and strived trying to find balance in diet, exercise and life, but failed miserably until I took hold of Romans 12:2: "Do not be conformed to the pattern of this world, but be transformed by the renewing of your mind" (NIV). I stopped relying on my flesh and let the Holy Spirit reign and have His way. His way looked much different than my way, for His way is the way of obedience.

I would quickly learn that the key to overcoming my flesh was death to self. I would learn to die to my desires to live to His. I felt like a child taking moment-by-moment instructions from her dad. I began to listen first instead of getting up and running out the door. I heard His voice calling me to Him. I learned that He was to be first in my life every day, before eating or exercise. I started asking Him, "Should I eat this or that?" I learned to have my time with the Lord first and then if I had time, I would exercise.

This way of thinking gave me such liberty, as it brought the right perspective to my life, and soon I was on my way to a balanced life. I also learned that the gym was not for me. I had spent half my life in a gym, and it brought imbalance to my life as I had the tendency to compare my body to others. I also stopped looking at fashion magazines, which was stumbling to my growth in the Lord and was a tool for the Enemy to use to take me down. I put 1 Corinthians 10:23 into practice, knowing that *all things are lawful for me, but not all things are helpful.* I began to feel free to exercise and enjoy it, no longer in bondage to it, realizing all along that all of these issues stemmed from my mind, and the answer

"All things are lawful for me, but not all things are helpful; all things are lawful for me, but not all things edify" (1 Corinthians 10:23).

to all my issues was found in renewing my mind by bathing in the Word of God daily.

Since, I have been able to go back into a gym setting and keep my focus on the Lord. I do prefer to exercise outside and love long walks on the beach trail with friends. However, the key for me is to keep my mind stayed on the Lord, in His word first, making Him my priority over exercise. This simple rule of thumb has proven helpful as it strengthened me to overcome several eating disorders early on in my walk with the Lord.

Not only did God's Word bring priority and balance to my life; it was preparing me for what was ahead. Reading the Word daily gave me purpose and passion like never before, because my focus had shifted from me to Him. As I prepared my heart daily, a heart with purpose developed into a heart for the Lord and for the lost. He began to give me His heart for others. I learned to pray, "Lord, let me see what you see, give me Your eyes for the hurting, Your eyes for the lost." I quickly found that when my eyes were off me and on Him, I became strong.

As we seek to love and serve the Lord, He will put His heart in us. What a beautiful thing! And when we hide God's Word in our hearts, He renews our minds and helps us develop balance, priority and perspective. For it's in hiding God's Word in our hearts that we recall: "Your Word I have hidden in my heart, that I might not sin against You" (Psalm 119:11).

We read of great men and women in the Bible who had purpose and passion and were used by God. Aside from their love for the Lord God, they each seemed to have the similar quality of a balanced life. Each of them purposed in their minds and hearts that they would not sin against God long before sin could enter. They were called to a high standard by God and used in great ways by Him.

Daniel is one who disciplined his mind, body and heart. He never put anything or anyone above the Lord in his life. We're told in Daniel 1:8, "But Daniel purposed in his heart that he would not defile himself with the portion of the king's delicacies, nor with the wine which he drank."

We also see this in Joseph, who purposed in his mind not to sin against God. Just before fleeing the advances of Potiphar's seductive wife, young Joseph asked, "How then can I do this great wickedness and sin against God?" (Gen. 39:9).

Ezra left the captivity of Babylon for Jerusalem, eager to teach his people. It was said of him, "For Ezra had prepared his heart to seek the Law of the Lord, and to do it, and to teach statures and ordinances in Israel" (Ezra 7:10).

Daniel, Joseph and Ezra are just three examples of godly men who prepared and purposed in their hearts to serve the Lord God, regardless of the cost. It's vitally important that we as believers are proactive, that we prepare and purpose in our hearts beforehand that we will not sin against God. The sooner we learn the dangers, temptations and challenges a Christian may face, the more equipped we become. There's much truth in an old saying, "Don't wait until you are thirsty to start digging a well!" The sooner we educate, the better. Don't wait until you're knee-deep in trials to start reading your Bible and praying. Be proactive and start now. Hide God's Word in your heart and you will be ready to handle the situation when it arises. You will be prepared to defeat the Enemy and the fiery darts he throws at you.

As I write this, I'm watching the most amazing thing take place outside my window. A Hawk is protecting its nest, sitting out in the open on a house as six or seven crows take turns dive-bombing this beautiful creature. The hawk just sits there and takes it, not moving at all, just standing watch over its nest. The hawk has purposed in its little mind that it will not move, no matter what, even with the constant attack from the enemy.

Likewise, we, too, can have this purpose of heart and mind and defeat any obstacle the Enemy places in our path. We can accomplish this is by being proactive in the Word, in heart and in mind. We must study God's Word to learn from the examples of those who endured the hardships, trials and temptations that we, too, face. Paul spoke of the sins and failures of the Israelites in the wilderness and warned the Christians at Corinth to learn from their example. He said, "Now all these things became our examples, to the intent that we should not lust after evil things as they also lusted" (1 Corinthians 10:6). Just five verses later Paul would write, "Now all things happened to them as examples, and they were written for our admonition, upon whom the ends of the ages have come." (verse 11). We are to learn from the successes and failures of those in scripture to help us prepare for situations we may encounter in life.

We also must purpose in our hearts early on by making a cognizant decision to stand upon our convictions so that when situations arise, our hearts will be purposed to serve God and not people. Making these decisions beforehand on how we will handle certain situations will help us when temptation arises. This produces a disciplined, balanced life that will grow stronger and stronger over time.

When we first got married, we vowed to never let the word *divorce* ever be uttered from our mouths. By the grace of God, all these years later, we have kept that promise because we purposed in our hearts long ago to not sin against God.

Joshua expected this behavior from the Israelites when he gave them his farewell address. He challenged them by saying, "Choose for yourselves this day whom you will serve" (Joshua 24:15). Making the decisions before the challenges arise will lead us to develop discipline, preparedness, and purpose of heart.

The mind is the Enemy's playground and an open doorway for temptation if given the opportunity. As Daniel purposed in his mind that he would not sin against God, we see that the decision begins long before the temptation arises. James shares with us how this temptation starts:

> Blessed is the man who endures temptation for when he has been approved he will receive the crown of life which the Lord has promised to those who love Him. Let no one say when he is tempted, "I am tempted by God;" for God cannot be tempted by evil, nor does He Himself tempt anyone. But each one is tempted when he is drawn away by his own desires and enticed. Then, when desire has conceived, it gives birth to sin; and sin, when it is full-grown, brings forth death" (James 1:12-15).

James says that sin always starts with a desire in the mind, then gives birth to sin, and when it's full-grown, it brings forth death. We must discipline our minds to be disciplined in our bodies. The only way that we can have a healthy mind is to center it upon the Word of God and the things of God.

One of the first Scriptures I memorized as a new believer was Colossians 3:1-5:

If then you were raised with Christ, seek those things which are above, where Christ is, sitting at the right hand of God. Set your mind on things above, not on things on the earth. For you died, and your life is hidden with Christ in God. When Christ who is our life appears, then you also will appear with Him in glory. Therefore put to death your members which are on the earth: fornication, uncleanness, passion, evil desire, and covetousness, which is idolatry.

When our minds are set on the things above, the things of earth grow strangely dim. Our priorities are suddenly reordered and our perspective on life is clear and no longer foggy.

Balance in the Christian life is key, but getting the balance is not easy. For me, this took many years of reprogramming. I spent twenty years sowing to my flesh, and it would take a good twenty years before I would fully understand that change *is*—and *is not*—dependent on me. It *is* dependent upon me in that the only thing that brings balance is the constant and continual reading of the Word of God. And it *is not* dependent on me in that I cannot change myself. Only the Holy Spirit can do that. Also worth noting is that we cannot change others. Only the Spirit of God can do that, so we must let go of control and spend time praying for others, which is much more productive.

The wonderful thing about forming the habit of putting Jesus first above anything or anyone is that before long you see results. At first, it's a fight to get there, but soon after, you will discover that much like brushing your teeth, you can't leave home without doing it! As you wash yourself in God's Word, you become clean, encouraged, enlightened, convicted and focused on what truly matters. It's not the housework or exercise that matters, it's *Jesus!* At times we may need a little reminder of the purpose to our time in the Word each day. Like with Martha, it wasn't that her working and serving were wrong. Rather, if she would have first sat and received from the Word, she then could have gone and serve her family and friends in the Spirit of God and not in her own flesh. The key is to make the decision to seek God first, and then the blessings will flow forth in and through our lives.

It's been said that if you go one day without God's Word, your family knows; go two days without God's Word, and your friends know; go three days without God's Word, and everyone knows! We may laugh at this, but the reality is that it's very true. I'm at the place in my life that I cannot go a day without being in the Word. I need it and I desperately depend upon it. I know that I have nothing to give out to others unless I have fresh "manna" each day.

You may remember in Genesis when the children of Israel complained because they didn't have any food. So God gave them manna, bread from heaven that was sweet like honey and melted in their mouths. But, they were also given strict instructions to only gather what they needed for that day. Then, they were to go back and gather fresh manna each day.

The Bible is our food, and we need fresh "manna" each day to survive. We cannot be sustained on yesterday's food, nor can we be growing spiritually on yesterday's manna. We need to be in the Word daily receiving from the Bread of Life and allowing it to be sweet like honey, melting in our mouths. The beautiful thing about God's Word is that it may at first, be difficult to acquire a taste for it, but as it goes in and begins to digest it sends nutrients to all parts of our bodies. And soon, we see our vital need for this manna. We cannot go without it for it is the only thing known to man that changes a person from the inside out.

Don't wait until you are thirsty to start digging the well. Be proactive like Daniel, Joseph and Ezra, who didn't wait until they were face-to-face with temptation to decide it's time to grow up spiritually. Be in the Word, in prayer, and in fellowship with the only One who can keep you from the snare of the Enemy. When we fail to invest the time to prepare ourselves spiritually, we prepare for failure.

Rather than set ourselves up for failure, why don't we learn to emulate these men and women in the Bible . . . men and women who prepared their hearts and minds ahead of time for the trials and temptations they would encounter along the way . . . men and women who made a difference in the Kingdom of God because they were proactive in their relationship with God?

Are you proactive in your relationship with the Lord? Are you purposing in your mind and heart, like Joseph and David, to not sin against God? Are you choosing, as Mary did. what is better?

Lord, help us to set our hearts and minds upon You today. Help us to purpose to know You more and to love You more so that we might not be overtaken or overcome by anything or anyone that may come our way.

9

Beaten but not Destroyed

~ learning to persevere ~

There are times in our lives when we may feel beaten up and battered, but not destroyed. We are in good company because Paul the apostle felt this same way. We're told in Acts 14:19 that Paul was stoned, dragged outside the city, and left for dead. But the church gathered around him and prayed, and he stood up and went back into the city where he had just been stoned to preach truth and proclaim the message of the gospel.

Many of us can relate to this on a smaller scale. Someone speaks unkindly about us or ridicules us, and we call it persecution. Today, most of us are ignorant of the real persecution that is going on in other parts of the world. People are being beaten, imprisoned and even beheaded for the sake of the gospel. Even though we can't relate to this type of brutal persecution, the Lord does at times allow us to feel a microscopic portion of the persecution that we read of in the Bible and see going on in other parts of the world. We need to ask the Lord *what* and not *why*: *Lord, what can I learn from this?* versus *Lord, why did this happen?*

Many people believe that the power of God manifested in and through a person's life should keep them from these difficulties. However, the reality is that the power of God working in and through a person's life actually brings conflicts and struggles. Paul the apostle is a great example of this. While on his missionary journeys, Paul endured many long and difficult trials. He was faced with fierce winds, poisonous snakes, beatings, stoning, ship wrecks, near drowning, and had a physical affliction that the Lord chose not to heal. The pressure on Paul was immediate, persistent and never ending, yet he always emerged victorious through the strength of Jesus Christ. Paul describes this for us in 2 Corinthians 4:8-10, saying,

> We are hard pressed on every side, but not crushed; perplexed, but not in despair; persecuted, but not abandoned; struck down, but not destroyed. We always carry around in our body the death of Jesus, so that the life of Jesus may also be revealed in our body (NIV).

We see in Paul's description above that he gives us five different images in succession. First is the picture of being completely surrounded by the Enemy who is pressing in but not crushing him. The literal meaning is, "We are crowded from all sides, but not defeated."

The second image is that of someone whose way is completely blocked or thwarted by the Enemy, yet he has just enough light to take the next step. Paul said, "perplexed, but not in despair" (NIV), or as one literal translation put it, "Without a road, but not without a side road of escape."

The third picture, "persecuted, but not abandoned," is one of the Enemy in hot pursuit of Paul while his divine Defender stands nearby. He is pursued but not left alone.

The fourth is even more vivid. The Enemy has now overtaken him, struck him, and knocked him down, but it's not a fatal blow. Literally it means "overthrown, but not overcome."

In the fifth and final image, Paul advanced the thought still further, giving us a picture that appears to be one of death itself: "We always carry around in our body the death of Jesus" (NIV).

Have you ever felt like this? The Enemy is in hot pursuit of you, crowding you, pressing in on you, persecuting you. You get beaten up a little, you are struck down, you may even be overthrown, but, you are not overcome . . . because of the cross, Jesus has already overcome the Enemy. You are victorious—Jesus has come to your aid.

I have only one experience so far in all my years with Jesus in which I felt "overthrown, but not overcome." As I was going through the battle, 2 Corinthians 4:8-10 was the Scripture passage that came to mind. I remember telling a friend that I had been "stoned" by the Enemy, but was still alive. For the first time I thought that maybe, just maybe, the Lord was allowing me to partake in a small amount

God has nothing worth having that is easily gained, for there are no cheap goods on the heavenly market.

of His suffering. It is times like this that many people grow discouraged and surrender instead of standing strong. They ask *why* instead of *what*. They don't see the trials of life as the appointments of God.

Regarding trials, persecutions and conflict, L.B. Cowman said:

> God has nothing worth having that is easily gained, for there are no cheap goods on the heavenly market. The cost of our redemption was everything God had to give, and anything worth having is expensive. Difficult times and places are our schools of faith and character. If we are ever to rise above mere human strength, and experience the power of the life of Christ in our mortal bodies, it will be through the process of conflict that could very well be called the 'labor pains' of the new life.[xi]

I like that: "*'labor pains' of the new life.*" This makes me think of Romans 5:3-4: "but we also glory in tribulations also, knowing that tribulation produces perseverance; and perseverance character; and character, hope." Hope is the expectation of coming good. The end of trials and tribulation should bring hope. We must have hope. If nothing else, as believers, we hope in heaven—at least we have that to look forward to! But God desires to use what the Enemy has intended for evil—our trials, our failures, and our persecutions—and use them for good to make us tenacious, determined, steadfast and purposeful.

I read a wonderful little book about the life of R. C. Chapman called *Agape Leadership*. In this book the author recounts the life of this wonderfully godly man, which many are unfamiliar with. Mr. Chapman was a kind and generous man who lived during the 1800s. He was considered by Charles Spurgeon to be the saintliest man he ever knew. He was also the mentor of George Mueller and a close friend of Hudson Taylor's. Chapman lived a humble life on the poor side of town, not because he had to, but simply because he wanted to. It was important to Chapman to live among those whom he was seeking to minister to so as to win them to Christ.

On one particular day the grocer of the local market became so upset with Chapman's open-air preaching that he spit on him. For a number of years, the grocer continued to attack Chapman. However, instead of returning evil for evil, Chapman sought to return good for evil. When Chapman's wealthy relative came for a visit he asked if he could buy him some groceries, and Chapman agreed—as long as the items were purchased from this particular grocer. After buying a large amount of groceries, the relative told the grocer to deliver them to R. C. Chapman. The stunned grocer told the man that he must have come to the wrong store, but the visitor explained that Chapman had sent him specifically to that store. Soon the grocer arrived at Chapman's house, where he broke down in tears and asked for forgiveness. That very day the grocer gave his life to Christ.

The key to winning our enemies to Christ is the love of God. "With lovingkindness," the Lord said, "I have drawn you" (Jeremiah 31:3). And through our lovingkindness, He will draw them to Him. Love covers a multitude of sins—if we truly love with the *agape* love of Christ. There is nothing anyone can do to us that we cannot forgive. In fact, the more we forgive, the greater the testimony.

May the Lord help us to overcome evil with good. We should ask, "How can I bless someone today? What can I do to return good instead of evil?" And, "Lord, what do you want to show me in all of this?" Remembering to ask *what* instead of *why* not only matures us, but also helps to keep our focus on the One who allowed the trial to begin with. Knowing that the Lord has meaning and purpose for all that He allows in our lives is both helpful and comforting.

Paul understood this concept as he was able to rejoice in tribulation knowing for certain that God was at work producing lasting character in him: "And not only that, but we also glory in tribulations, knowing that tribulation produces perseverance; and perseverance, character; and character, hope. Now hope does not disappoint, because the love of God has been poured out in our hearts by the Holy Spirit who was given to us" (Romans 5:3-5).

The longer we walk with the Lord, the more we will see that He truly has a plan for everything that happens in our lives. He sees and allows all circumstances in life. Nothing happens by accident with God. Rather, everything is divinely orchestrated by our loving Heavenly Father. He has a purpose, and He will strengthen us to make it through anything that He places in front of us. And one day, we will be able to say, as Paul did, "We glory in tribulations" (Romans 5:3).

I think the following stanzas from this poem sums it up beautifully:

Once I heard a song of sweetness,
As it filled the morning air,
Sounding in its blest completeness,
Like a tender, pleading prayer;
And I sought to find the singer,
Whence the wondrous song was borne;
And I found a bird, quite wounded,
pinioned by a cruel thorn.

I have seen a soul in sadness,
While its wings with pain are furl'd,
Giving hope, and cheer and gladness
That should bless a weeping world
And I knew that life of sweetness,
Was of pain and sorrow borne,
And stricken soul was singing,
With its heart against a thorn.

Ye are told of One who loved you,
Of a Saviour crucified,
Ye are told of nails that pinioned,
And a spear that pierced His side:
Ye are told of cruel scourging,
Of a Saviour bearing scorn,
And He died for your salvation,
With His brow against a thorn.

Lord, may we learn to bring You glory in our times of trials, trusting that You are indeed building perseverance, character and hope in us, always helping us to seek to what and not why?

10

Alone in the Battle

~ learning to walk in victory ~

There are times in our Christian walk when we feel alone. Nobody likes this feeling, and as a result, we often murmur and complain to the Lord, saying, "No one understands us, our life, our feelings, our vision, our purpose, our conviction, our passion . . . and I am left alone."

I've felt this way many times in the ministry, surrounded by people yet still feeling all alone. Have you ever walked into a crowded room, and felt all alone? Well, you aren't alone, although the devil would love you to think otherwise. I'm encouraged that many in the Scriptures felt this same way. Knowing that we are not alone, but Jesus is right there with us, is comforting.

Elijah was one who knew well what alone meant. After experiencing a great victory on Mount Carmel, he was threatened by the wicked Queen Jezebel. Elijah ran for his life and a manhunt began. He hid in a cave and complained to the Lord that he was all alone, and none were left who had not forsaken the Lord. But Elijah was wrong. He didn't see as the Lord saw; he could only see his current circumstances. And it took Elijah running for his life and hiding all alone in a cave to see the unseen. Little did Elijah know that the Lord had reserved not fifty, or one hundred, or even four hundred, but He had kept seven thousand priests safe and sinless who had not bowed the knee to Baal.

We often lose perspective when we're on the run. We can overreact, take things personally, and isolate ourselves. We can easily forget God always has a reserve. He always has someone, even if it's just one person, who knows how we feel and has walked down the same road as we are walking, and they are stronger because of it. It is in these dark times that God is ever present.

It was during a dark time of loneliness and exile on the Island of Patmos that John received the vision of heaven and of things to come. It was during his time alone, with no one else there, that Jesus showed up and met John and ministered to him. If John had never been alone in that place of seclusion, we may never have received the book of Revelation. And it's when we are in our dark, lonely times, that Jesus shows up and ministers to us through His Spirit. It's nice when we can have someone with skin on to comfort us. But we must remember Jesus is the only One who fully understands, and He has promised never to leave or forsake us.

David understood this well. He was a godly young man, brave and bold. He was a man after God's own heart. David was familiar with being alone. He was out in the field alone with the sheep as his older brothers went to battle. David was ridiculed, belittled and looked down upon by his own brothers even after Samuel anointed him as the new King. But David didn't let that stop him, because God had called him as at a young age and prepared him for what lay ahead.

One day as his brothers were out to battle against the Philistines, David was asked to take them some supplies (see 1 Samuel 16-17). As he drew close, he heard the loud sound of the huge man—the giant Goliath. He stood ten feet tall and had six fingers on each hand. I'm sure he was scary to look at. But David wasn't afraid; he trusted the Lord, who had helped him in the past. Unlike his brothers, who ran *from* the battle, David ran *to* the battle and was confident in who God made him to be and what God created him to do.

David knew that God was with him and upon him. He walked in victory because God had prepared him long before. David had fought and killed lions and bears in preparation for Goliath. The Lord prepared David for what was ahead. He allowed him to defeat smaller enemies before the big one.

Likewise, He allows us to experience being alone in the battle like Elijah and David. He allows us to lack confidence so that He might show Himself strong. He prepares us for the task at hand by defeating smaller enemies before we get to the giant. He gives us unconventional weapons for the battle. For David, it was a slingshot and smooth stones. For us, it is prayer and the Word of God. Be diligent to use the weapons God has given you to defeat your enemy.

For though we walk in the flesh, we do not war according to the flesh. For the weapons of our warfare are not carnal but mighty in God for pulling down strongholds, casting down arguments and every high thing that exalts itself against the knowledge of God, bringing every thought into captivity to the obedience of Christ, and being ready to punish all disobedience when your obedience is fulfilled (2 Corinthians 10:3-6).

This war we wage as believers is a spiritual one that can only be fought with spiritual weapons. We may not have a slingshot or smooth stones, but we do have a sword. This is our sharpest and most effective weapon in the battle. The Word of God is the only piece of armor used both offensively and defensively.

This war we wage as believers is a spiritual one that can only be fought with spiritual weapons.

When Jesus was tempted by Satan for forty days in the wilderness, He used His sword—the Word of God—to fight each temptation that was thrown His way. There is power in the Word of God. That's why the devil will try his hardest to keep you from it. Know that when you are tempted to skip reading the Bible for a day or two that your sword is growing dull, and you will soon be overtaken. Instead, sharpen your sword and be ready for the attacks of the Enemy. Then, you will be able—through the Word, your sword—to take out any foe that comes your way.

I recall one particular summer when there was a heavy and continual attack on my family. The Devil was trying to take us out. He was relentless, and I was beside myself. I was praying and reading the Word, I even called a few close friends for prayer support. One day, I was outside having a conversation with the Lord, and out of my mouth came these words for all to hear, I said: "You cannot have him. He belongs to Jesus." There was power and authority in my voice as I spoke out against the Enemy on behalf of my family. I felt instant peace and victory. The war was over, and the battle won. I learned a great lesson that day, which is that oppression is very real and requires us to go into battle mode.

We must fight for our families, we must labor in prayer, and we must slay the Enemy with our sword, the Word of God. Know the Bible inside and out. Know the power given us by the Holy Spirit. Know the tactics of the Enemy, and be ready to fight. The more we are a threat to the Enemy, the heavier the attacks. The same power that was given to David and Elijah is available to us. We must use that power, depend on it, cling to it, and say it out loud! There is incredible power found in the name above all names—the name of *Jesus*. Say it. Sing it. Speak it. Pray it. The name of *Jesus* causes the Enemy to flee.

I have learned that it is also good to have a few trusted, likeminded people for prayer support. If you are under attack, don't isolate yourself from believers. Ask for prayer support from godly people. Grab your sword and go into battle mode. Don't run from the battle, just as David did not run from it, because there is no armor on your back, and you will be taken out. Seek the Lord diligently, and confidently, speak out against your Enemy. Know that God has purpose in your loneliness. Keep your sword sharp, because the victory has already been won at Calvary. So take it!

11

High Places and Nets

~ learning to obey ~

In reading through 2 Kings, there is a repetition among the "good kings" verses about those who "did evil in the sight of the LORD." We're told that the good kings, which weren't many, "did what was right in the eyes of the LORD." But, "the high places were not removed." Again and again we read this. Why? Why did they not obey the Lord and tear down the places of idol worship? How could they obey the Lord in some things and not all? Did they think that it wouldn't affect them? I wonder if any of these kings who called themselves followers of the Living God were really sold out for the Lord?

As I pondered this, the Lord quickly reminded me of my own walk with Him, and the times when I obeyed the Lord halfheartedly, partially obeying Him to remove from my own life the things that hindered my fellowship with Him. Just like these kings, I loved the Lord and worshiped Him, but there were some things that stood in the way.

I allowed idols to remain that should have been thrown out when I got saved. Much like Achan in Joshua 7, who took spoil from Jericho and hid it under his tent. I thought I could keep certain things and no one would know. But I neglected to consider the fact that God sees and knows all and nothing is hidden from His sight. Jesus shared in Luke 8:16-18 about the parable of the revealed light. He said,

> "Now no one after lighting a lamp, covers it with a vessel, or puts it under a bed; but sets it on a lampstand, that those who enter may see the light. For nothing is secret that will not be revealed, nor anything hidden that will not be known and come to light. Therefore take heed how you hear. For whoever has, to him more shall be given; and whoever does not have, even what he seems to have shall be taken from him."

When we become Christians and begin walking in the light, we need to realize that certain things need to go or these things can end up hindering us. Achan ended up hindering a whole nation as he sat on the idols hidden under his tent. He took from the spoil, thinking no one would know, but he forgot that God sees and knows all.

God loves His kids so much that He will bring those things that we try to hide into the light so as to reveal our sin and draw us to repentance. God is a jealous God, and He doesn't want anything in the lives of His kids to take priority over our relationship with Him. He said to the Children of Israel, "You shall have no other gods before Me. You shall not make for yourself a carved image—any likeness of what is in heaven above, or that is in the earth beneath, or that is in the water under the earth; you shall not bow down to them or serve them. For I, the Lord your God, am a jealous God" (Exodus 20:3-5).

There are many people who call themselves Christians, but in reality, they don't understand that to be a Christian means that you are a follower of Christ. And to follow Christ, you have to count the cost, and counting the cost often means getting rid of things or people that may hold us back and hinder our relationship with the Lord. We may not carry around statues these days, but we do carry around devices—smart phone, computers and tablets—all of which have the potential to draw us in and take valuable time away from our calling (see *Redeeming the Time* sidebar).

An idol is simply anything or anyone placed above the Lord. Jesus wants to be number one in

Redeeming the Time

According to Entrepreneur magazine, experts estimate from recent studies that time spent on social media is on the rise. While the average person spends more than five years' worth of screen time in a lifetime, that same person averages a little over a year socializing with family and friends in real life over their lifetime. But there are extreme averages, among which teenagers are said to log in nine hours a day. According to the founder of Common Sense Media, that figure reflects "the sheer volume of media technology that kids are exposed to on a daily basis." To grasp how this is affecting how we redeem the time, consider reports that show a giant leap in time spent on social media: Facebook users rose from 5 percent in 2005 to 68 percent in 2016.

Earlier statistics show that we spend over four hours a day on our mobile phones, one year and ten months on our lives, not number two or number three or number ten. This takes discipline and constant refocusing of our attention and energy toward the Lord. We live in a digital age, where we are constantly stimulated and distracted. We wake up each day with our phones nearby, and many plug in first thing. Tony Reinke, author of *12 Ways Your Phone is Changing You*, wrote, "My phone is a window into the worthless and worthy, the artificial and the authentic. Some days I feel as if my phone is a digital vampire, sucking away my time and my life.

YouTube, over a year on Facebook and Snapchat, eight months on Instagram and under a month on Twitter. Those totals, which have since grown in proportion to an increase in users, reflected more than five years spent on social media. This is in addition to some fifteen years spent watching TV, nourishing and grooming our bodies, socializing and doing laundry.

The five plus years spent on social media alone is the equivalent of flying to the moon 32 times, walking the Great Wall of China 3.5 times, climbing Mount Everest 32 times, running 10,000 marathons, and walking our dog 93,000 times.

See then that you walk circumspectly, not as fools but as wise, redeeming the time, because the days are evil. Therefore do not be unwise, but understand what the will of the Lord is.

Ephesians 5:15-17

Other days, I feel like a cybernetic centaur—part human, part digital—as my phone and I blend seamlessly into a complex random of rhythms and routines."

Some questions we must ask ourselves are: *What effect does technology have on our spiritual life? What is it producing in me and out of me? Is my phone changing me and others for the better? Do I have balance with technology? Does it rule me? Do I find myself overcome with comparison? Am I harnessing the opportunity to get the gospel out and encourage others in their walks? Am I grabbing the attention of my virtual audience in effort to glorify God or am I caught in the current and being carried away?*

When Jesus called Peter, Andrew, James and John to be His disciples, He asked them to do only two things: one, drop their nets, and two, follow Him. This seems easy enough. But upon further investigation into the lives of these men, we realize that their nets represented their livelihood. All these men knew was fishing; it was the family business. To leave it all behind meant they had nothing to fall back on, and that's exactly what Jesus wanted: 100 percent of them—no turning back.

Many of us have yet to drop our nets and follow Him wholeheartedly. A net can be represented by fear, addiction, money, a relationship, pride, inadequacy, imbalance, or occupation. Whatever it is, the call remains the same as it was with Peter, Andrew, James and John: "Follow Me and I will *make* you *become* fishers of men" Mark 1:17, emphasis added). I love that Jesus *makes us become* knowing good and well that we cannot do it ourselves. He is there to help us, to see us through, to strengthen us, to change us, challenge us and test us.

This process of becoming fishers of men is one that we see and read about in the lives of the disciples. Peter is the most spoken of, making the most blunders and yet becoming the leader of the Early Church. He was impulsive, and impatient, yet confident and courageous. This gives me hope. The Lord loves to use the "nobodies" to become "somebodies" for Him. That way, He's sure to get the glory. I may be a nobody, but in the eyes of my Savior I am a "somebody."

Paul tells us in 1 Corinthians 1:27, "God has chosen the foolish things of the world to put to shame the wise." He delights to use us that He might get the glory. It seems that in my own life I have learned the most when I have failed. When I have made big mistakes and have suffered the consequences.

I recall one time when I was painting the boys' bedroom late at night, and John suggested that I go to bed. I was adamant to finish the room. He walked by sometime later and saw the can of paint sitting on the ladder. He said, "You should probably move that before you spill paint all over the carpet."

Of course, I didn't move it. And, yep, I knocked it over spilling bright orange paint all over the off-white carpet! I began praying out loud to God, pleading for help to remove the stain and for intercession so John wouldn't be mad. Specifically, I asked the Lord for forgiveness for not listening to my wise husband! Praise God, the stain came out with several applications of stain remover and the rental of a carpet cleaner. I have since learned to listen to my husband's warnings.

Normally, when I have a check in my Spirit, it's because something isn't right, and I have a choice to go with that check or not. I've discovered that the more I listen to and obey that check in my heart, the more easily I hear it and obey it the next time. Becoming familiar with the voice of God takes knowing His voice, and knowing His voice takes time, intimacy and obedience. This often requires dropping those things that can hold us back, setting down the phone and picking up the Bible, to follow Him, trusting that *He will make us become* whatever it is that He has called us to.

The key when following Jesus is not looking back. The enemy loves for us to look back, but Jesus wants us to look forward to what He has prepared for us from the foundations of the earth. Look forward today to the glorious hope that Jesus has prepared for those who trust and obey Him.

For the grace of God that brings salvation has appeared to all men, teaching us that denying ungodliness and worldly lusts, we should live soberly, righteously, and godly in the present age, looking for the blessed hope and glorious appearing of our great God and Savior Jesus Christ, who gave Himself for us, that He might redeem us from every lawless deed and purify for Himself His own special people, zealous for good works. Speak these things, exhort, and rebuke with all authority. Let no one despise you (Titus 2:11-15).

12

Living Love

~ learning agape love ~

Love is defined perfectly for us in 1 Corinthians 13: 4-8: "*Love* suffers long and is kind; *love* does not envy; *love* does not parade itself, is not puffed up; *love* does not behave rudely, it does not seek its own, is not provoked, thinks no evil; does not rejoice in iniquity, but rejoices in the truth; bears all things, believes all things, hopes all things, endures all things. *Love* never fails."

Now remove the word *love* and put your name in its place. You don't get very far, do you? Now put in Jesus' name instead of the word *love* and see how far you get. Amazing, isn't it? It's a perfect snapshot of Jesus! "God is love" (1 John 4:8), and Jesus is God. So Jesus is the very definition of love. Loving people isn't easy. In fact, it's really hard. I remember hearing

Pastor Chuck Smith say, "We're not called to like the sheep, we're called to love them!"

Love is really what sets us apart as believers. We love each other, we love others, and we love Jesus.

Peter, one of Jesus' closest disciples and the one who was the boldest and most courageous in his faith, shared openly about his great love for Jesus. Peter said he was ready to die with Jesus and would never deny Him. But even brave, bold Peter denied Jesus. How could this happen to such a strong and determined man? How could Peter, who said he would die for his faith, turn on Jesus? It started with pride and moved to following at a distance, then warming himself at the enemy camp, which finally lead to three denials. Let this be a lesson to us, to not be prideful and arrogant or impulsive in our faith. Let us also learn from Peter that if we are going to follow Jesus, that we must follow Him closely and steer clear from the enemy camp, lest we, too. deny Him. We may not say that we don't know Jesus, as Peter did, but we can certainly show with our life and actions whether we are following Him closely.

After Peter denied Christ three times, he repented and was publically restored by Jesus Himself on the shore of the Sea of Galilee. And just as Peter denied Jesus three times, Jesus asked Peter three times in John 21:20: "Do you love Me?"

Peter responded, "Yes, Lord, You know I love You." Jesus asked the same question each time, and Peter responded the same way each time. At first reading, all looks good. But if we were to read the Greek word for *love* that Jesus was using, it changes everything.

There are three well-known Greek words for love: *eros, phileo* and *agape. Eros* is the word we ordinarily see in classical Greek writings and describes the love between a husband and wife.

Phileo is a broader word, generally used for the love of friends. It speaks of a kindly, affectionate love and is used for the love shared by a parent with a child. It can even speak of a love for one's country.

The last kind of love is *agape* and is used for a higher type of love, a love that is all-absorbing, a love that completely dominates one's being. This is the word that Jesus was using when He asked Peter if he loved Him. Peter's response was the same each time: "Yes, Lord; You know I *[phileo]* you."

Peter had grown fond of Jesus, he was affectionate toward Him, and he loved Him as a child loves his parent. But Jesus wasn't using that term for love. Jesus was saying to Peter, in essence, "You said you were willing to die for Me. Are you really willing to express a self sacrificing love that is absorbed in others and not yourself? Do you love Me like that, Peter?"

Peter, knowing the word that Jesus used, answered in a manner of speaking, "Lord, you know I'm fond of You and think of You like a parent whom I've let down and is now disappointed in me."

Jesus, in hearing Peter's response, did not rebuke him, nor does He disqualify him from service. Jesus instead commissioned Peter into service.

I love that Jesus didn't say, "I'm sorry Peter you are disqualified from service, you don't love me to death yet."

But Jesus, knowing all, knew what Peter would become. He knew Peter would eventually turn from shifting sand into a solid rock on which the church would be built. Peter would one day be able to respond with, "Lord, I *agape* You" as he laid down his own life for Christ, being crucified upside down for his great love for Jesus.

What was it about Peter that took him from *phileo to agape*?

I believe there were six specific milestones that took place in Peter's life that we can learn from and that brought about his almost overnight transformation.

The first is *humiliation*. Peter needed to be humbled. He was prideful and over confident and ended up falling. But he also was repentant. And when he saw Jesus on the shore, he (in classic Peter form) jumped into the water and swam to Jesus (see John 21:7).

Second, we see Peter's public *restoration,* found in John 21:15-17. Jesus asks Peter three times, "Do you love me?"

Peter reaffirmed three times with, "Yes Lord, You know I love You."

Three questions for three denials . . . a coincidence? I think not.

Third, we see that Peter was *commissioned.* After Jesus restored Peter, He commissioned him into service, saying, "Feed my lambs" (verse 15); "Tend my sheep" (verse 16); and "Feed my sheep" (verse 17).

Three commissions for three denials . . . coincidence? No, I don't think so.

Fourth, we see that Peter was given *instruction.* In John 21:18-22, we see that Jesus shared with Peter the death he will die. And Peter—still learning quickly—replies with, "What about this guy, Lord?" (speaking of John).

Jesus said, "If I will that he remain until I come, what is that to you? You follow Me."

Fifth, we see that in just ten days, Peter is filled with the Holy Spirit in Acts 2:1-4, which was the milestone of *infiltration.* As evidence of this, the disciples spoke in tongues, and Peter immediately stood up and addressed the multitude on the day of Pentecost, preaching a Spirit-filled sermon that resulted in three thousand people getting saved.

The final stop on Peter's long road to *agape* love was crucifixion, just as Jesus had prophesied. This would prove Peter's all-absorbing, self-sacrificing love for Jesus Christ.

So how do we go from *phileo* to *agape?* The same way Peter did. If we truly want to live the love of 1 Corinthians 13, we need to walk along the same road as Peter. Oh, it may look a little different for us. We may not have to die on a cross, but we will need to die to our flesh, our will, our way and our desires to put Him and others first. We may not get to lead three thousand people to the Lord, but we all are called and commissioned by Jesus to share the gospel message to those who will listen. Also, the Lord may not tell us how we're going to die, but we do know where we are headed when we die. We may not have Jesus prepare us breakfast on the Shore of Galilee, but He promises to never leave us. We may not be beaten or put in prison, but we're certain to experience trials and tribulations just the same.

The strongest trees are not found in the thick shelter of the forest but out in the open, where fierce winds bear down from every direction bending and twisting tree trunks and limbs into giant,

The strongest trees are not found in the thick shelter of the forest but out in the open ...

strong and durable full grown trees. These trees are sought by toolmakers for their tool handles because the wood is good, thick and strong. Likewise, when you're out in the open serving the Lord and getting hammered by the winds of trials, be encouraged that the Lord Jesus is making you into a strong handle for His mighty tool.

Jesus knew what it would take for Peter to go from shifting sand to solid rock. And He knows what it takes for us to learn how to love as we should. He often puts people in our life to help sand our rough edges. Some of those people may even live in our own homes. Nevertheless, He empowers us with His Spirit to learn to love as He loved:

> Beloved, let us love (*agape*) one another, for love(*agape*) is of God; and everyone who loves (*agapes*) is born of God and knows God. The one who does not *love* does not know God, for God is love (*agape*) (1 John 4:7-8).

Knowing the true definition of God's love really changes everything, doesn't it? God's love is not self-seeking; God's love is self-sacrificing. God's love is not self-absorbed; God's love is Christ-absorbed. God's *agape* love is completely unselfish and the only way that this is even possible for us, as it was for Peter, is to be filled and refilled by the Holy Spirit each day.

Unless we draw from the power of the Holy Spirit, we cannot love the way Jesus commands us to love. It's an exchange. I choose to set down my way of trying to love and take up His. I relinquish my rights and surrender to Him. I ask Him to fill me with His power to love, and He does! Romans 5:5 affirms this: "The love (*agape*) of God is shed abroad in our hearts by the Holy Spirit who was given to us."

The most important quality in our lives as Believers is *agape* love. It should set us apart from the world. It's the first fruit of the Spirit listed in Galatians 5 and is more important than any gift we ever could be given by God. Without love, our gifts are useless, and as Paul says, they are loud and obnoxious, like a clanging symbol (see I Corinthians 13:1).

If my husband John were to give me a gift, throwing it at me with an attitude, I really wouldn't want it. But if he were to wrap it in beautiful wrapping paper and put a nice, big bow on top and then present it kindly and affectionately, I would be excited to receive it. Love is the beautiful bow that ties all the gifts together, and without it, those gifts are loud and obnoxious.

Do you want to grow in love? Then spend more time with the Author of love. When John and I fell in love, we spent every moment together that we could. We learned about each other and grew together, and now we even know what the other is about to say. Jesus wants you to know Him that intimately. He already knows what we will say before we say it, but He wants us to know what He would say and how He would respond and how He would love. Get to know Him, and He will rub off on you!

May the Lord empower us with His Spirit and enable us to love (*agape*) Agape like He loved!

13

Depression, a Real Enemy

~ learning how to fight it ~

I like to think of myself as a positive person. I am rarely shaken by circumstances, but when I am, it hits me hard. There have only been a few times so far in all my years as a Christian that I've been hit with depression. It was always a major melt down that prompted my depression: a miscarriage, a move, or a division. Each time I reacted the same way in that I ran to Jesus to hold me, comfort me, and sustain me. I looked to the Scriptures for comfort and direction and allowed myself time to grieve before moving on. I have found the longer I dwell on a situation or circumstance, the easier I can go to that place of depression. The key for me has been to get back to the people of God and the work of God. There is something about serving others that gets our eyes off ourselves and onto others.

Often, after a great victory or an incredible mountaintop experience, we can find ourselves in a valley, a low place—a place that, if we are not careful, and if we allow ourselves to dwell there too long, can take us into the pit of despair. Elijah is a prime example of this. He defeated the false prophets of Baal on Mount Carmel in a stunning display of God's power (see I Kings 18). But instead of being encouraged, Elijah, fearing Jezebel's revenge, ran for his life. Weary and afraid, Elijah allowed himself to go to a place that I imagine he never thought possible.

Depression is the feeling of severe despondency and dejection, and affects how we feel, think and act. Depression causes feelings of sadness and loneliness that results in isolation. The Enemy wants to isolate us so he can harass us and lie to us. If we begin to believe his lies long enough, we can place ourselves in danger of harm. Depression can, and often does, lead to thoughts of self-harm and even suicide. Suicide is reported as the second cause of death in those aged fifteen to twenty-five. This is a huge problem some are calling "an epidemic of hopelessness."

Now may the God of hope fill you with all joy and peace in believing, that you may abound in hope by the power of the Holy Spirit (Ephesians 5:15-17).

He (Elijah) came to a broom bush, sat down under it and prayed that he might die. "I have had enough, LORD," he said. "Take my life; I am no better than my ancestors." Then he lay down under the bush and fell asleep (1 Kings 19:4-5 NIV).

How could this happen to a man who has been used so greatly by the Lord? How could he waver so quickly? Here we see the flesh—the human side of Elijah, which I'm so grateful is revealed with many other examples in the Bible. Even though the Bible doesn't use the word *depression,* it does use words such as *downcast, sad, forlorn, discouraged, downhearted, mourning, troubled, miserable, despairing and brokenhearted.*

Depression is very real, and it can strike anyone. David, Hagar, Moses, Naomi, Hannah, Elijah, Job, Paul and even Jesus all struggled with depression at one time or another. Depression strikes rich people like Solomon and poor people like Naomi, old people like Job and young people like David, women like Hannah and men like Jeremiah. Depression affects believers, non-believers, and backslidden believers.

It's often something that we don't discuss in the church due to embarrassment or not really knowing what it is. Depression can follow after a time of victory or after times of defeat, but it is always a tool of the Enemy. He will promote self-pity and feelings of loneliness and discouragement. He will also cause you to dwell on your circumstances and become paralyzed by your situation.

David experienced this type of depression on many occasions. He found himself alone and depressed in the cave of Adullam (see 1Samuel22:1-2). When his family heard about his state of mind, they went down to be with him. The Scriptures tell us that everyone who was in distress, in debt, and those who were discontent, gathered to him. So he became the captain over four hundred men. A distressed David, surrounded by men who were in debt and discontent. You would think this would equal bad company for one struggling with depression. However, the company was exactly what David needed to get his eyes off himself and onto others. David cried out to God in Psalm 142, and he asked for help and deliverance for himself and for those with him. When we face depression, we must not isolate; we must infiltrate. We must push past the paralyzing fear and doubt and dig deep within ourselves to offer up praise and prayer in the midst of our pain.

In David's case, this wasn't the end of feeling downcast. David experienced depression on more than one occasion. 1 Samuel 30 gives us another such account:

> When David and his men reached Ziklag, they found it destroyed by fire and their wives and sons and daughters taken captive. So David and his men wept aloud until they had no strength left to weep (verses 3-4 NIV).

This was a distressing time for the people and for David. His wives and children were taken too, and the people talked about stoning David. So, what did David do? He sat down and wallowed in his situation? No! David did the opposite. He did several things that we can learn from to bring himself and his people out of this depressive state.

First, David strengthened himself in the Lord, as their leader seeking God in preparation (see verse 6).

Next, he went to Abiathar, the high priest, and asked for the ephod, the garment of praise and worship. Then, he inquired of the Lord through prayer as to whether he should go to battle or not.

Finally, David heard from the Lord and obeyed His voice, therefore performing what God had instructed: "So David inquired of the Lord, saying, 'Shall I pursue this troop? Shall I overtake them?'

And He answered him, 'Pursue, for you shall surely overtake them and without fail recover all' (verse 8).

David did what was right by *preparing* himself as he sought the Lord in the Word first. Next, he put on the ephod, which was a garment of *praise,* making a conscious choice to praise and worship the Lord. He also spent time inquiring of the Lord in *prayer.* Finally, David obeyed God. This often means getting up as David did and going back to *perform* in the battle.

If we choose to do these things, we are sure to be lifted from our state of depression. In times of darkness and depression, I have had to make a conscious choice to prepare my heart by seeking God and praising Him in the midst of the storm.

This alone is helpful, but as with David, many were watching his every move, looking to him as their leader. We, too, are leaders. Some of us are leaders at church and in ministries, some are leaders at work or in the home. We all are leading someone, somewhere as believers, because people are watching us, and they never watch so closely as when we go through a storm.

Get into the habit of looking for the silver lining in the storm clouds. Don't yield to the discouragement that proceeds depression. A discouraged soul is in a helpless state, neither able to stand against the wiles of the Devil nor able to prevail in prayer for others. L. B. Cowman wrote, "Flee every symptom of the deadly foe of discouragement as you would run from a snake. Never be slow to turn your back on it, unless you desire to eat the dust of bitter defeat."[xii]

Discouragement has the potential to quickly take us places that, like Elijah, that we thought we would never go. Instead of dwelling on it, run from it. Make a conscious choice not to let it take you down but to take you into the presence of God. Grab your Bible and mark up all the promises of God. Receive His promises and let the Word sink deep within your heart. Fix your eyes upward instead of inward, and be strengthened. As soon as you choose to wholeheartedly turn away from discouragement and your lack of trust, the Holy Spirit will awaken your faith and breathe life into your soul once again.

The choice is ours either to look up and be renewed or to lay low and wallow in discouragement.

It's always a danger for an eagle to fly too low because that is where the poachers wait and where an eagle can meet its death in the lowlands. However, an eagle who soars high in the sky reaches safety and freedom from the attacks of its enemy. So too, if we choose to keep our eyes up (on Jesus), we always will rise above any circumstance, looking for the good in the storms instead of letting them take us out. If we, like Joseph, let the Lord turn what the Enemy has intended for evil in our lives and use it for good, we always will rise above our circumstances and experience the most growth.

Certain plants and flowers experience the most growth in the darkest times of the night. Indian corn never grows more rapidly than in the darkness of the warm summer nights. The evening primrose will not open in the sunlight but waits to reveal its beauty as the evening grows darker. This is the case with us as well. We often shine our brightest, as believers, when we're in the darkness because we know that God has a plan and purpose in it.

I experienced this when I had a miscarriage between the births of our second and third sons. Although I was just eleven weeks along, my body went into labor for an hour to release the baby. I felt alone and could not understand why God would allow this. I just wanted to share the details with someone of what I saw and experienced. I was full of emotion and extremely hormonal. And right in the midst of my turmoil and pain, Jesus showed up and held me like I've never experienced before or since. He gave me instant peace and comfort so thoroughly I didn't want that feeling to end. It was so sweet and tender and something that is forever etched into my mind. But I still wondered why. Why would God take a child from me? Had I done something wrong? Was I being punished?

For many weeks and months I struggled with this. I cried a lot and had a difficult time reading the Bible and worshiping at church. I couldn't focus at all. All I could do was cry. But in my suffering, I was reminded of the arms that held me and ministered to me.

One day several months afterward, I was at my neighbor's house. She shared with me that she had just miscarried her baby. I was able to comfort her with the comfort that was given to me. I shared Scripture verses with her and prayed for her. Just that alone helped me tremendously in my recovery. I felt like God revealed to me that He truly did have a plan and purpose for what He allowed in my life. I was blessed to really be able to feel her pain and then to comfort her. Jesus made it possible for me to give her hope for the future and in the process, He gave me hope, too. A few months later, we both were pregnant again. She gave birth to a beautiful little girl and I had our third boy!

The Devil would love nothing more than to strip us of all hope, to make us feel hopeless and as though life is not worth living. When we.re depressed, we don't expect anything good. We find ourselves caught in a downward spiral of self-pity, which can often lead to medication. As we make the choice to seek God face-to-face, we're magnificently lifted from our pit of despair, and people watch in amazement as our lives reflect a peace that surpasses all understanding with supernatural strength.

There are many Scripture passages that have comforted me in my low times of depression. Here are a few verses that I hope will comfort you as well:

The LORD Himself goes before you and will be with you; He will never leave you nor forsake you. Do not be afraid; do not be discouraged (Deuteronomy 31:8 NIV).

Have I not commanded you? Be strong and courageous. Do not be afraid; do not be discouraged, for the LORD your God will be with you wherever you go (Joshua 1:9 NIV).

The LORD is close to the brokenhearted and saves those who are crushed in spirit. (Psalm 34:18).

"So do not fear, for I am with you; do not be dismayed, for I am your God. I will strengthen you and help you; I will uphold you with my righteous right hand" (Isaiah 41:10 NIV).

"For I know the plans I have for you," declares the LORD, "plans to prosper you and not to harm you, plans to give you hope and a future. Then you will call on me and come and pray to me, and I will listen to you" (Jeremiah 29:11-12 NIV).

"And I will pray the Father, and he shall give you another Comforter, that he may abide with you forever" (John 14:16).

[Jesus said,] "And surely I am with you always, to the very end of the age" (Matthew 28:20).

For we live by faith, not by sight (2 Corinthians, 5:7NIV).

And not only that, but we also glory in tribulations, knowing that tribulation produces perseverance; and perseverance, character; and character, hope. Now hope does not disappoint, because the love of God has been poured out in our hearts by the Holy Spirit who was given to us (Romans 5:3-5).

God allows trials to come our way to mold us into His image, but the Devil will often use our trials to take us into a pit of depression. Don't listen to the lies of the Enemy. Instead, let the trials take you higher.

L.B. Cowan wrote about this in "Streams in the Desert": "The sufferings of this life are God's winds. Sometimes they blow against us and are very strong. They are His hurricanes, taking our lives to higher levels, towards His heavens."[xiii]

I like that: our trials are God's hurricanes, taking us higher. Living in Florida for ten years, we experienced a few hurricanes, and they are not fun. The power often goes out, trees fall down and people panic. We're the same way with the trials of this life. We often panic and fall down instead of letting the trials take us higher.

One of the first rules of aerodynamics is that flying into the wind quickly increases your altitude. The wings of a plane create more lift by flying against the wind. The same is true with birds. If a bird is simply flying for pleasure, it flies with the wind. But if a bird senses danger, it turns in to the wind to gain altitude and flies up toward the sun.

What a great visual for us, given by the Creator of the universe: turn in to the wind and fly up to the Son—the Son of God that is! Fall upon the truth found in the Word of God. Make yourself pick up the Bible and read it. Make yourself go to church. Make yourself serve others. Make yourself . . . soar higher. If you do these simple things, you will soon find that you're no longer depressed, and your focus has been restored.

Make a conscious choice, like David, to *prepare, praise, pray* and *perform*, remembering that you are more than a conqueror in Christ Jesus! Get out there and get moving, and go against the wind if necessary to rise above your circumstances. God is building a great testimony in and through your life, and He desires to get the glory.

14

Unattractive Wrappings

~ learning to trust ~

Trust is the ability to rely on the character, capacity, strength or truth of someone. Trust is earned, and it's something that is gained over time, but can be lost in a moment. D. L. Moody said, "Trust in yourself and you are doomed to disappointment, but trust in GOD and you are never to be confounded in time or eternity."[xiv]

Recently, I read a devotional that got me thinking. There are certain lessons from the Lord wrapped in unattractive paper. Lessons we have to learn that aren't pretty—and may even appear downright ugly from the outside. But when the ugly wrapping is pulled back, layer upon layer, the beauty of the package on the inside is revealed. It's that old saying, "Don't judge a book by its cover." Well, in this case, it's don't judge a gift by its wrappings.

Have you ever been at a Christmas party where there is a white elephant gift exchange? Does anybody really know what one of those is anyway? Is it a joke gift, a used gift, or a gift under $10? Regardless, when I choose a gift, I usually go for the one with the nicest wrapping. But that's not always a good indication of what's inside. Oftentimes the *white elephant* is an old sock or broken coffee mug. But with the Lord, it's often the other way around: ugly, detestable wrapping covers a beautiful priceless gem on the inside. The Bible says, "Man looks on the outward appearance, but the Lord looks on the heart" (I Samuel 16:7).

"Man looks on the outward appearance, but the Lord looks on the heart" (I Samuel 16:7).

This is the case with diamonds found in the rough. In an unpolished state a diamond's beauty is unseen. In natural form a diamond is an unassuming gray stone most people would ignore. But this gray stone becomes a thing of beauty after a skilled gemologist unveils its potential. The most magnificent diamond in the history of the world was found in an African mine and was presented to the king of England to embellish his crown. The King sent the jewel to Amsterdam to be cut by an expert stonecutter. The expert took the stone of priceless value and cut a notch in it. Then he struck the gem with a hard hammer blow, and the majestic jewel fell into his hand, broken in two.

Most of us would look at this act as careless and foolish, but what we fail to see is that the expert studied and planned for days, even weeks, how with exactly one blow of the hammer, he would create not only one but two magnificent stones. Only in the hands of a skilled professional could this be accomplished. The highly skilled stonecutter saw what others couldn't see. He saw the full potential of the diamond. He saw that deep within the diamond lay two priceless stones.

Likewise, the Lord alone can see our diamond in the rough. He sees our full potential. He allows a stinging blow to fall upon us. We feel the pain and agony of discomfort and think, *This must be a mistake.* But it's not. God allows discomfort and pain to form us into the most precious jewels in the world, because He is the most skilled stonecutter in the universe. And one day, when He's done with His chiseling and hammering, we'll be beautiful jewels adorning the crown of the King of Kings.

God's "stone cutting" is a lifetime process, one that we never will completely arrive at until we are in glory with Him. Trials may come at unexpected times in unexpected wrappings, but inside something beautiful is developing. I imagine that nobody viewed the cross as an attractive wrapping. None of Jesus' followers understood the cross until later. Jesus tried to tell them—He tried to explain heaven to them and the place that He was going to prepare for them, but they couldn't grasp the concept. They only understood the here and now, not the then and there. To the followers of Jesus, the cross was a dull gray stone, but to God, the cross represented a double diamond inside. Jesus would not only die to save sinners from hell, but He would go ahead to prepare our beautiful mansion in heaven—a double blessing, an unexpected diamond in a stone of gray.

Oh that we could have His eyes to see the plans and purposes He has for us. His plans are good, "plans to prosper you and not to harm you, plans to give you a hope and a future" (Jeremiah 29:11).

Lord, help us to see our full potential and to trust You as our skillful craftsman while You chisel and hammer away . . . all to reveal the beautiful diamond inside.

15

Be Still and Know

~ learning to wait on God ~

The Bible has a great deal to say about waiting on God. We read of many men and women in the Bible who had to wait on the Lord for a promise to come to fruition. We read of Abraham and Sarah, Joseph, Moses, Elijah, Noah, David, Daniel, Esther, Paul, Mary and even Jesus Himself had to wait on God for His perfect timing to come to pass. We often become impatient with God's delays. Yet much of our trouble in this life is the result of our restlessness. We grow weary in our waiting and often begin to move ahead of God instead of continuing to wait. In "Streams in the Desert" L.B. Cowan wrote, "We cannot wait for the fruit to ripen but insist on picking it while it's still green."

Waiting is not an easy task. In fact, it's one that I've been working on for many years. Of all the spiritual disciplines in my life, this one I have found to be the most difficult. Waiting takes time. It means that we are patient and that we trust the Lord for His perfect timing and not ours. God's waiting room means we are often still and silent with little or no movement at all. The Psalmist knew this well, because he wrote in Psalm 46:10: "Be still and know that I am God."

God's waiting room means we are often still and silent with little or no movement at all.

David was a shepherd, musician, mighty warrior, fugitive, king, husband father and man after God's own heart. Though David was constantly on the move and had great responsibilities, he knew the vital importance of stillness before Almighty God, waiting on Him, and listening intently to what the Lord would say to him. David found comfort in the waiting, as well as direction, wisdom and worship. We, too, can have this same relationship with God—if we will stop long enough to be still.

To be "still" means "to be free from disturbance, commotion and agitation, to remain in place at rest, motionless, stationary." I don't know about you, but this doesn't describe me at all. I'm constantly on the move with my husband, our family, chores, the ministry, and all the responsibilities that my life entails. But the Lord desires that I would come to Him, just like David, and be still and listen. Strength is found not in the busyness and noise, but in quietness, stillness and solitude. Birds travel in flocks, dogs travel in packs, but the

lion and the eagle are usually found alone. This same strength
is available to us if we would just come to Him.

David spent much time in solitude and he recorded many
of his conversations with God for us in the Psalms. The life
of David serves as an example to us that we, too, can have an
intimate relationship with Jesus if we are willing to *be still* and
listen instead of just speaking. Sometimes we forget that the
Lord is waiting, wanting to speak to us, and it's easy to miss
this opportunity every day. When we finally do understand, as
David did, the great blessing of being still and listening to the
still, small voice of God, we will never want to leave.

Waiting on God in solitude is vital to see Him and receive
vision from Him. And the amount of time spent before Him
is also critical. As we spend time, still before God, to listen to
Him and bask in His presence, waiting becomes like developing
film. Our hearts are like the film—the longer they're exposed,
the deeper the impression. For God's vision to impress upon
our hearts, we must sit in stillness at His feet for a while. Have
you ever noticed that water has to be completely calm for you
to see your reflection? Any slight movement in the lake or
river, and your image vanishes. The reflector must be still, as
with our hearts when seeking the Lord, for in the stillness of
time and space the very reflection of God is revealed.

There are many in the Scriptures who saw a form of God,
and the result was always the same: a transformed life. Jacob
crossed the ford of the Jabbok (Genesis 32:22), saw God, and
was transformed into Israel. Gideon was transformed from a
coward into a courageous soldier when he saw a vision of God.
In the New Testament in Acts, Thomas was changed from a
doubter to a loyal follower after seeing the risen Savior for

himself. William Carey, the English missionary of the eighteen and early nineteenth centuries, considered by many to be the Father of modern missions, saw God and left his shoemaker's bench to go to India. David Livingston saw God and left everything behind in Great Britain to become a missionary and explorer through the jungles of Africa during the nineteenth century.

If we want to "see God" and be transformed like these men were, then we need to be in a place where we can see His reflection—a calm place, a place of solitude, a place alone with Him. If we want to be used by God, we need to spend ample time alone with Him, receiving from Him, basking in His presence, listening to Him, and waiting upon Him in stillness. Even Jesus found it necessary to withdraw from people for brief periods of time to be alone on a hilltop with God. If Jesus found it necessary, how much more do you and I need the solitude, away from distractions and crowds, to listen to the still, small voice of our Savior?

I've found my times of solitude with Jesus to be sweet and priceless. The times I am able to just bask in His presence or lay out prostrate in complete submission have proven to deepened my faith and trust in the One whom my heart longs to be with. No amount of money can buy such peace, serenity and love that the Father has for His kids. He beckons us to Him. He calls us daily to be still and know that He is God. Why don't we hear? Why don't we listen? It's because we are too busy, our minds are too clouded, and our schedules are too full to stop and take the time to hear from the Creator of the universe, the One who loves us so very much—our Abba Father.

It's when Joseph was alone in the pit and the prison that God spoke. It's when Abraham was alone on Mount Moriah about to sacrifice his son in obedience that God spoke. It's when Elijah was alone and on the run that God spoke. It's when Adam and Eve were alone hiding that God showed up. It's when Jacob was alone, wrestling with God, that God touched his hip and blessed him. It's when David was alone, trying to cover his sin, that God spoke through Samuel. And it's when Jesus was alone, in the Garden of Gethsemane, sweating drops of blood, that God spoke and confirmed His will. God speaks whenever and through whomever He wants. The question is, are we listening?

When Elijah was on the run from Queen Jezebel and was hiding in a cave, we read that there was a great wind and earthquake and fire . . . and then a still, small voice. First Kings 19:11-15 tells us,

> Then He said, "Go out, and stand on the mountain before the Lord." And behold, the Lord passed by, and a great and strong wind tore into the mountains and broke the rocks in pieces before the Lord, but the Lord was not in the wind; and after the wind an earthquake, but the Lord was not in the earthquake; and after the earthquake a fire, but the Lord was not in the fire; and after the fire a still small voice.
>
> So it was, when Elijah heard it that he wrapped his face in his mantle and went out and stood in the entrance of the cave. Suddenly a voice came to him, and said, "What are you doing here, Elijah?"

> And he said, "I have been very zealous for the
> LORD God of hosts; because the children of Israel
> have forsaken Your covenant, torn down Your altars,
> and killed Your prophets with the sword. I alone am
> left; and they seek to take my life."
>
> Then the LORD said to him: "Go, return on your
> way to the Wilderness of Damascus; and when you
> arrive, anoint Hazael as king over Syria."

It's often when we're on the run, hiding from God, or fearful that God will show up and speak in profound ways. As with Elijah, God let him run and run and run until he couldn't run any farther, and then He showed up and spoke to him. But this was only after He had gotten Elijah's attention with some greater acts of nature: an earthquake, a fire, and severe wind. After Elijah was wide-eyed and attentive, God spoke very softly in what was described as a whisper. How beautiful is that! Our God will allow us to run and allow things to in our lives that are big and loud and dangerous—all to bring us to the place where we will be still, wide-eyed, and attentive to His whisper! Our God is a good God, a loving God, a kind and affectionate God . . . a God who speaks. Won't you take the time today to listen to His still, small whisper? He loves you so very much!

The next thing we see after God spoke to Elijah is that He told him to get back to the work of the Lord. The Enemy loves to use fear to take us out of the service of the Lord. God had seven thousand people reserved whom Elijah knew nothing about. That's seven thousand people who had not bowed the knee to Baal. God has resources that we know nothing about, and He often will reveal to us bits and pieces of His plan so that we might get up and get back into the race as not to become disqualified.

We have many distractions in this life, many things that are constantly pulling and tugging on us. It may not be fear that the Enemy uses. Rather, it may be the busyness of life that he uses. I believe this is why stillness before God is such a great discipline, and one that seems to go unmarked with believers today. Think about it. When was the last time you were still before God and took time to stop and listen? When did you last hear His whisper?

We, too, just like David, can dialogue with the Lord. He waits for us to come and be still and listen to His still, small whisper. Many do not hear from the Lord because they are unwilling to do what it takes. When you sit down to your devotions, come expectantly, bring a pen and journal in hand, and see what He might say to you. You'll be so encouraged as the Lord speaks to you, in His Word and in the stillness of His whisper. Listen carefully, without distraction or commotion, and He will speak. Then, write it down! The more you listen, the more He speaks. Bask in His presence, kneel at His feet, and enjoy sweet communion with Jesus.

"Be still and know that [He is] God" (Psalm 46:10). As you are still, motionless and quiet, He will make Himself known to you. It's a promise—go take it!

16

Running to Win

~ learning endurance ~

I must admit, I do not enjoy running. I tried to like it in college when I took a running class just for fun, but ended up sick to my stomach after running ten miles. I don't ever remember experiencing that runners' high people talk about, although there was a time in my life when I enjoyed getting out of the house, away from the kids for a quick run with the dog, to pray, clear my mind and gear up for the rest of the day with my little kiddos. I looked forward to that time each day or so to regain perspective, to breathe the air outside, to feel free and not cooped up, and to enjoy the fact that I could still run for exercise and not just run after kids.

One thing I learned about running is that it takes discipline to continue to run and motivation to even get started. It's easy to do a quick sprint here and there. But the key, once you get started, is building your endurance, going a little farther each time, pushing yourself, and pressing on a little more for your body to respond to what your mind is saying.

Running is similar to the Christian walk. We have to be motivated toward a goal to get started and disciplined to continue to push ourselves further each day. We may begin walking and then jog, and finally we are running with a prize in mind. For some this is a donut, for others it's a healthy blended smoothie, and still others it's the simple satisfaction of knowing they can still actually run! Whatever the motivation, the fact remains the same: discipline and determination are the keys.

Paul wrote in Philippians 4:13, "I can do all things through Christ who strengthens me," and he shares with us many times in his epistles about running. I believe that Paul was also the author of Hebrews, which says,

> Therefore we also, since we are surrounded by so great a cloud of witnesses, let us *lay aside* every weight, and the sin which so easily ensnares us, and let us *run with endurance* the race that is set before us, *looking unto Jesus,* the author and finisher of our faith, who for the joy that was set before Him endured the cross, despising the shame, and has sat down at the right hand of the throne of God (Hebrews 12:1, emphasis added).

As the return of Jesus draws closer and the signs of the times draw near, we look to God's Word for comfort, encouragement and motivation to continue the race that He has set before us. Hebrews 12:1 gives us certain conditions for running with endurance.

First, we are to lay aside the weights and sin that can hinder us. This is a key factor in our race and one that can determine how fast or how slow we run and also how consistent or inconsistent we run. To "lay aside" means "to discard, abandon and shelve." When we see runners in the Olympics, we don't see weights attached to them, and we'll never see them dragging something behind them. In fact, they make it a point to not even allow extra clothing to keep them from performing their best. We'll even from time to time see some long distance runners running barefoot so as not to hinder their race.

As believers, we're encouraged to *abandon* anything that or anyone who may minutely weigh us down or hinder our race. It may be sin that we've allowed to remain in our lives for a time, and this, too, can hinder our race. Our new life in Christ is not to be one of dragging around the old man or woman. It's to be one of running strong and free from those things that used to weigh us down.

There was a time when I held on to some old baggage way too long—five years too long. As a new believer, I was ignorant of many of the things of Christ. But as I drew closer to Jesus and read the Word more, things became clear about what Jesus intended for me—the joy, peace and purpose from a life following after Him. I began to see that the things I thought were God's will for my life were hindering my walk and slowing me down. What a joy it was to set down the baggage and begin to run my race in life with freedom. He set me free—and I was free indeed, free to grow, free to serve, free to live an unhindered life in Christ.

The Enemy loves to keep us in a place of bondage, which slows us down in our pursuit of godliness. Jesus died to give us an unhindered life in Him, but we have to make the conscious choice to obey. Obedience is a key for any athlete. I can either choose to obey the instruction of my coach or not to obey it. It's all up to me. Do I want to become a better athlete or not? Do I want to grow in the Lord or not? Obedience often takes sacrifice.

For me it was a relationship, sin, and many other smaller things that had a hold on me. This didn't happen overnight. It took years of the Lord revealing various hindrances here and there. Again, it was my choice whether to obey and be teachable or not. I'm not sure why it's so hard to let some things go when I knew that it holds us back. I had to lay it down and set it aside to move forward in my walk and focus on the Lord. Also, I had to determine in my mind to stay focused on Jesus and no longer be tripped up by the things I had laid down.

Focus is another condition we are given for running our race: we are to *focus* on Jesus, who set the example for us to follow. We're told to *look to Jesus, the author and finisher of our faith, our race.* He is the author of our lives, our race. He is the finisher of our race—we don't have to run the race alone. He has already run the race beforehand and also runs with us. I always enjoyed running with others, as it seemed to make the time pass more quickly. When I run alone, I have to concentrate on something other than the run so as not to think of the pain I'm in or the fact that I have barely run a mile! Personally, I like to listen to good uplifting music to forget that I'm running and pushing all my muscles beyond what they are capable of. I concentrate on remaining focused on anything other than my run. I'm sure this is not the correct way to run for exercise, and I definitely don't recommend it. What I can recommend though, is remaining focused on Jesus instead of yourself— that will help you tremendously!

Finally, we are to *endure*, which means to remain, last, continue, abide, persist, persevere—and my favorite—survive. Sometimes all we can do is survive! Certain seasons of our race are almost unbearable, and we may feel we are doing all we can to survive. We often don't have energy to take another step, let alone run. What can we do then? We continue . . . we hang in there, persist, and persevere We keep doing all we can . . . we don't give up. Why? Because we are not running alone. Jesus is right there with us, and He has run the race before us, so He's familiar with what it takes to run to the finish!

What does your race look like? Are you sprinting? Are you dragging? Have you given up and stopped, thrown in the towel? Paul would say, "Run with endurance the race that is set before you." Each of our races are going to look a little different. My race includes my family, extended family, church family, and a whole lot of ministry. I'm constantly challenged to remain focused on my race, to finish well, to run strong, and to remain consistent. These things are across-the-board the same for all believers. But where we differ is in our approach and technique. Am I jumping the gun by a false start? Have I slowed down because I'm looking back? Have I ended up in someone else's lane? Or worse yet, have I become disqualified?

So many different factors make up this race called life. Some are in difficult situations. Some are struggling in their marriage, some have a disease and their days are numbered. Even though we all are running in different lanes, we're all running for the same purpose, with the same prize in mind, and this must be our focus. We must focus on the prize, the upward call of Christ Jesus that we may not become tripped up by the tactics of the Enemy, who is relentless in his pursuit. Jesus came for one purpose, and that was to die for humanity. While on earth He ministered and healed, but His calling, His purpose for being born, was to die for the sins of the world.

We are also called--called to make His death known, called to share the message of His death with the world, called to bring hope to the hopeless and comfort to the brokenhearted. Before Jesus ascended to heaven He left His disciples with a command, a commission:

> "Go therefore and make disciples of all the nations, baptizing them in the name of the Father and of the Son and of the Holy Spirit, teaching them to observe all things that I have commanded you; and lo, I am with you always, even to the end of the age" (Matthew 28:19-20).

God has commissioned us to spread the good news of the gospel message. But weights and sin and compromise can get in the way and even prevent us from sharing if we aren't running our race well. We are not to run as the world runs. Our race should look very different from theirs. Not that we won't have struggles, trials and tribulations, but because He has overcome the world, we, too, are overcomers and don't have to bend with the pressure to resemble the world.

We are to resemble Jesus. The closer we run with Him, the more we resemble Him. The closer we run with Him. the more focused we are on His call for our life. The closer we run with Him, the more effective we are for the kingdom of God. We run to receive a prize. Our prize is a crown, a crown that we can cast down at the feet of Jesus. A crown that cannot be found here on earth, a crown that will be rewarded in heaven as we stand before the Lord, and He says the words that we all long to hear: "Well done, good and faithful servant, enter into the joy of your Lord." As we stand before the Lord, we will take our crowns that we receive and cast them down at the feet of Jesus. What a blessed event that will be!

This is why we run with such endurance. We have this blessed hope to look forward to! We press on, press in and look up as we run because we are focused on the crown that we get to cast down at the feet of the One who died for us. This is why we endure our race. This is why we stay in a difficult marriage . . . this is why we continue in prayer for our prodigals . . . this is why we serve the Lord . . . this is why we never give up . . . this is why we don't give in to the temptations of the world. We persevere until the end. May the Lord grant us all we need to stay focused and not give up in our pursuit of the crown.

We must remain constant keeping a light touch on things and people, not letting anything weigh us down. We must endure, persevere and remain focused on Him until He comes or until He takes us home, whichever comes first. After all, what runner enters a race to lose?

Do you not know that those who run in a race all run, but one receives the prize? Run in such a way that you may obtain it (1 Corinthians 9:24).

This race is ours to run, so let's run to win!

Author's Note

Michelle Randall is a gifted Bible teacher, speaker and author. She has led women's Bible studies for over 20 years. Her love for the Word of God has inspired her to minister to, disciple and encourage all women to share her passion for Jesus. Michelle's husband, John Randall, is the senior pastor of Calvary Chapel San Juan Capistrano, where she leads the weekly women's Bible Study and heads up the women's ministry, *Calvary Women*. Michelle and John married in 1992 and are the parents of four children.

If this book has encouraged you in your walk, then I would love to hear from you. You can follow me on Instagram @Michellerandall1, calvarywomen.net, or send an email to michellerandall@ccsjc.com.

Jesus said, "I am the way, the truth and the life. No one comes to the Father except through Me" (John 14:60).

If you have not given your life to Jesus, it is my prayer that you would receive Him into your heart today as your Lord and Savior. He is the only way to true happiness, joy and peace. He is the only way to heaven.

I invite you to respond to His great love for you today and begin your journey with Jesus. And remember—your journey, like mine, is a work in progress that will continue until you are face-to-face with Jesus in glory.

It is not so much what we can do for Jesus, but what He has done for us that transforms our lives from broken vessels into wholesome vessels to be poured out for His use. Keep your eyes on Jesus, read God's Word daily, stay in fellowship with other like-minded believers, and attend a good, Bible teaching church.

As you remain steadfast in your faith, abounding in the work of the Lord, you will be amazed at how the Lord transforms you into His image.

Only be strong and very courageous, that you may observe to do according to all the law which Moses My servant commanded you do not turn from it to the right hand or to the left, that you may prosper wherever you go" (Joshua 1:7).

References

Chapter 5: My Father, the Gardener

[i] Cowman, L.B., *Streams in the Desert: 366 Daily Devotional Readings,* ed. James Reimann, s.v. "September 19" (Grand Rapids, MI: Zondervan, 1997), 356.

[ii] Ibid.

[iii] Quoted in William MacDonald, *Believer's Bible Commentary* (Nashville: Thomas Nelson, 1989), 900.

[iv] Charles Spurgeon, quoted in L.B, Cowman, *Streams in the Desert*, s. v. "December 12," 461-462.

[v] Spurgeon, Charles H. *Faith's Checkbook* (Chicago, Moody Press, 1987), 119.

Chapter 6: Great Faith Tested

[vi] Meyer, F.B. "Beside the Drying Brook," *BibleHub.som*, accessed April 16, 2014, http://biblehub.com/sermons/auth/meyer/beside)the?drying?brook.htm.

Chapter 7: Discipline, the Hard Surrender

[vii] Elliot, Elisabeth. *Discipline: The Glad Surrender* (Grand Rapids, MI: Fleming H. Revell, 1982), 15.

[viii] Ibid.

[ix] Elliot, Elisabeth. *Discipline.* 24.

Chapter 8: The Balancing Act

[x] OxfordDictionaries.com, s.v. "balance," accessed May 3, 12014, http://www.oxfrddictionaries.com/definition/english/balance.

Chapter 9: Beaten but Not Destroyed

[xi] Cowman, L.B. *Streams in the Desert*, s. v "June 29," 254-255.

Chapter 13: Depression: A Real Enemy

[xii] Cowman, L.B. *Streams in the Desert*, s.v. "April 2," 138.

[xiii] Ibid. "February 4," 61.

Sidebar: Depression:

Chapter 14: Unattractive Wrappings

[xiv] Quoted in *Record of Christian Work*, vol. 19, eds. Alexander McConnell, William Revell Moody, Arthur Percy Fitt (East Northfield, MA: W. R. Moody, 1900), 767.